PASTA DISHES

Numerous ideas for making the most of wholewheat pastas –
dishes made from wholefood ingredients in exciting
combinations.

PASTA DISHES

by

JANET HUNT

Illustrated by Clive Birch

THORSONS PUBLISHERS LIMITED
Wellingborough, Northamptonshire

First published May 1982
Second Impression October 1982

British Library Cataloguing in Publication Data

Hunt, Janet
    Pasta dishes.
    1. Cookery (Macaroni)
    I. Title
    641.8'22   TX809.M17

    ISBN 0-7225-0750-X

Typeset by Glebe Graphics, Wilby, Northamptonshire.
Printed and bound in Great Britain by
Richard Clay (The Chaucer Press) Ltd.,
Bungay, Suffolk.

CONTENTS

Wholefoods, quite simply, are foods in their natural state – nothing added, nothing taken away. In this age of mass-production foods, wholefoods are not always easy to obtain. But as nutritionalists and doctors become increasingly convinced of their value in building and maintaining health, so their availability is fast improving.

Include as many natural, unadulterated foods as you can in your day to day eating pattern, and discover not just exciting new tastes and a fresh approach to mealtimes, but better health too.

PASTA, THE FAMILY FAVOURITE

Nowadays, most people buy their pasta ready-made. Wholewheat varieties, made without colouring or preservatives, are available at health food and wholefood shops, and include the popular spaghetti, lasagne and macaroni as well as more unusual (but equally delicious) shapes such as caramelle and tagliatelle. Some pastas also include eggs in their ingredients, others have spinach added to colour them green. But the basic ingredient is durum wheat, a very hard wheat grown in North America and Italy, which provides all the natural nutrients of the whole grain including protein, and the vegetable dietary fibre now known to be essential to good health.

The slightly nutty flavour of wholewheat pasta blends well in most recipes, and as it is more satisfying than pasta made with refined ingredients, and contains only approximately 100 calories per dry ounce, it is an ideal food for slimmers. (If pasta has the reputation for being a fattening food, blame the sauces served with it!) Most people find two ounces is an ample portion, although the Italians tend to need four ounces each to satisfy their appetites – probably because they eat the refined white pasta!

To cook your wholewheat pasta, bring a large pan of salted water to the boil, add the pasta slowly, (especially spaghetti which needs time to soften so it will curl round to fit into the pan), and cook fairly briskly, without a cover, for ten or twelve minutes. Your pasta is ready to use when it is tender but still firm – the expression usually used is *'al dente'*, and the best way to

judge if it is cooked is to bite it! Wholewheat pasta does not need
to be rinsed, but is simply drained, and dressed with a little
vegetable oil or polyunsaturated margarine, ground black
pepper, and the sauce of your choice. If you are using the pasta
in a salad, however, it should be rinsed in plenty of cold water,
then set aside to get completely cold, and can be forked
occasionally so that it does not stick together. Lasagne, too, is
best rinsed in cold water to prevent further cooking before it is
made up into the recipe you are following, and put into the
oven. It can, in fact, be made up two or three days before
needed, and kept covered in the fridge, as can any pasta. To re-
heat cooked pasta that is *not* going to be further baked, just
plunge it into boiling water, bring back to the boil, then drain
and use immediately.

Home-made pasta is nowhere near as complicated as people
seem to think, though it does depend what shape you want the
finished product to take. *Gnocchi* is the easiest pasta of all to
make as it does not need to be rolled out or filled. Making your
own noodles, or pasta strips for lasagne, cannelloni or ravioli is
also relatively quick and simple. (It is now possible to buy pasta
machines which make the job even easier.) Traditionally,
though, pasta comes in a huge range of shapes including stars,
shells, bows and wagon wheels; and in a range of sizes from tiny
seeds to wide ribbons. Once you have learned how to make the
basic pasta dough you may like to experiment with some of
these artistic varieties (and maybe understand why the spaghetti
maker is considered an artist in Italy!).

Cook and use your home-made pasta in the same way as the
ready-to-use kind, and preferably soon after you have made it –
the fresher the better. The basic dough recipe given here
includes sea salt, but some cooks feel it is preferable to omit this
in the dough, as the salt in the water will be sufficient. Try it both
ways.

How you serve your home-made or shop-bought pasta is
entirely up to you. The following recipes show how versatile it
can be, and hopefully they will give you the courage to go ahead

and find more new ways to dish up this super-value wholefood. Any soup can be made more filling with the addition of pasta; use a tiny amount of vermicelli if you want to make your soup more interesting without making it *too* satisfying. Try any of the dishes here as a main course, or halve the amounts given and serve them as a starter, Italian style. Use whatever pastas you have handy – it isn't necessary to stick to the ones suggested, and a different variety may make all the difference to the recipe! Don't forget you can use pasta for sweet dishes, too. Macaroni pudding is a traditional dish, but not many people think of serving other pastas for dessert. Nevertheless, the bland taste and soft texture of pasta go well with yogurt, cream, fruit, and the crunchiness of nuts, and can easily be sweetened if desired.

One final point: because pasta is traditionally served with cheese or cheese sauces, many of the recipes given here follow that basic pattern. This doesn't, of course, mean they cannot be used by vegans – sauces can be made with soya milk, thickened and made creamier with tofu; nuts can be sprinkled over the top instead of cheese.

Margarine, when specified, can be a vegan variety, or can usually be replaced by vegetable oil without changing the final taste too much. (In fact, with the current controversy about low-cholesterol margarines, it might be a good idea for everyone interested in building good health to use more oil and less margarine.)

Once you've grown used to making and cooking pasta, you'll find it invaluable – as well as a favourite dish with your family. So read on, and then get cooking. Good appetite!

All recipes are for 4 people.

MAKING AND COOKING PASTA

BASIC DOUGH FOR PASTA

1 lb (450g) plain wholemeal flour
2 large eggs
Water to mix
Sea salt to taste – optional

1. In a bowl sieve together the flour and salt.

2. Make a well in the centre and pour in the two lightly beaten eggs; add just enough water to bind the ingredients and make a firm dough.

3. On a floured board knead the dough until smooth and elastic; if possible, allow to stand for a short time before proceeding.

4. Divide the dough into smaller amounts, and roll out as thinly as possible – the thickness of paper is ideal, but this takes practice.

5. Then use according to the following variations.

RAVIOLI

Roll out the dough and cut into small pieces about 1½ in. square. Add filling to each one, cover with another dough square, and seal edges firmly.

Alternatively, you can roll out one large piece of dough, mark it into squares, and put some of the filling mixture in the centre of each one. Then cover with a second large sheet of dough and press firmly around the filling before cutting into squares. Although this is the more traditional way to make ravioli, dough made from wholemeal flour is more likely to break than that made from the more glutinous refined flour, so handling large sheets of dough can cause problems.

CANNELLONI

Roll out the dough into rectangles about 5 in. x 4 in. and cook in boiling water before adding filling. Then roll up and place in greased ovenproof dish, cover with a white, cheese or tomato sauce, and bake in the oven.

TAGLIATELLE

Roll out the dough into large very thin rectangles, flour lightly, then roll up loosely into a sausage shape. Cut with a sharp knife into ¼ in. strips. Unroll before using them – they can be left to dry if not required for immediate use.

NOODLES

Make as for tagliatelle, but cut strips much thinner.

LASAGNE

Roll out the dough as usual, then cut into long wide ribbons about 2 in. x 8 in. As lasagne is used in baked dishes it must be cooked in boiling water first, and is then layered with the filling of your choice.

PASTA VERDI

You can colour your pasta the traditional and attractive green quite easily. Cook 2-3 oz (50-75 g) fresh spinach, *purée* it, and drain very thoroughly. Add this to the basic dough as you add the eggs, then proceed as usual.

WHEAT GERM PASTA

Substitute 2-3 oz (50-75 g) wheat germ for flour, sieving it together with the remaining flour before adding the eggs, and adjusting the liquid content in order to get the desired consistency.

BUCKWHEAT NOODLES

2 oz (50 g) plain wholemeal flour
6 oz (175 g) buckwheat flour
1 egg
Water to mix
Sea salt to taste – optional

1. Combine the two flours in a bowl, then add the salt.

2. Add the lightly beaten egg.

3. Gradually stir in enough water to make a firm but pliable dough.

4. On a floured board knead the dough until smooth and elastic.

5. Divide the dough into two pieces, then roll out as thinly as possible; dust with a little more flour.

6. Set aside for an hour or so to dry out.

7. Roll each piece of dough up to make a sausage shape; then use a sharp knife to cut into very thin strips. Do not press too hard or the dough will stick together.

8. If you wish to cook the noodles immediately, unroll them, then drop into boiling salted water and simmer for 10 minutes. Rinse before adding other ingredients.

9. If they are not for immediate use, unroll the noodles, then set aside to dry. (As they do not contain any preservatives, they cannot be kept for long).

SOUPS AND SALADS

TOMATO SOUP WITH NOODLES

1½ lb (675 g) tomatoes
2 onions
2 carrots
2 pints (1.1 l) vegetable stock
2 tablespoonful vegetable oil
4 oz (100 g) wholewheat noodles
½-1 teaspoonful sage
2 tablespoonsful plain yogurt – optional
Seasoning to taste

1. Heat the oil in a pan; add the chopped tomatoes, onions and carrots; *sauté* for 10 minutes, turning occasionally.

2. Pour in the stock with the sage and seasoning; bring to the boil; simmer for 30 minutes.

3. Sieve or *purée* the soup, then return to pan and add the noodles; cook for 10 minutes or until the noodles are tender.

4. For a creamier texture, stir in the yogurt; serve at once.

MINESTRONE

4 oz (100g) haricot beans, soaked overnight
2 pints (1.1l) vegetable stock
1 clove garlic, crushed
2 tablespoonsful vegetable oil
2 onions
2 celery stalks
2 carrots
1 turnip
4 tomatoes
½ small cabbage
2 oz (50g) wholewheat macaroni
1 tablespoonful tomato *purée*
1 teaspoonful oregano, or to taste
Chopped parsley
Grated Parmesan cheese
Seasoning to taste

1. Heat the oil and toss in the finely chopped onions and garlic; *sauté* for a few minutes.

2. Wash, peel, and slice or dice the celery stalks, carrots, turnip and tomatoes; shred the cabbage.

3. Add the celery, carrot and tomato to the pan and *sauté* until just turning golden; pour in the stock; tip in the drained beans, tomatoes, tomato *purée*, herbs and seasoning.

4. Boil for 10 minutes, cover the pan and simmer for 45 minutes.

5. Add the macaroni and cabbage and continue cooking for about 20 minutes more, or until the beans and macaroni are tender. (You may need to add more liquid, although this is a thick, chunky soup, so don't water it down too much.)

6. Adjust the seasoning; serve topped with freshly chopped parsley and grated cheese if liked.

LEMON CHOWDER

1 oz (25 g) polyunsaturated margarine
1 oz (25 g) wholemeal flour
1 pint (550 ml) milk
1 pint (550 ml) vegetable stock
1 large onion
1 large green pepper
6 oz (175 g) fresh or frozen sweet corn
3 oz (75 g) wholewheat spaghetti rings
1 lemon
1 small carton soured cream
Chopped chives
Seasoning to taste

1. Melt the margarine in a pan; add the finely sliced onion and pepper and cook for 5-10 minutes or until beginning to soften.

2. Stir in the flour and brown over a low heat.

3. Pour in the milk and stock; season; bring to the boil, stirring continually.

4. Add the pasta and simmer, covered, for 10 minutes.

5. At the same time, cook the sweet corn in a separate pan until just tender.

6. Add the drained corn to the pasta with the juice and grated rind of the lemon; stir in the soured cream and heat gently for a few minutes (do not let the soup boil).

7. Adjust the seasoning and serve sprinkled with chives.

MISO SOUP

1 tablespoonful vegetable oil
2 pints (1.1l) water
2 tablespoonsful miso, or to taste
1 large onion
1 large carrot
1 or 2 strips wakame or dulse seaweed
Florets from a small cauliflower
3 oz (75 g) wholewheat macaroni or spaghetti, broken into
  pieces
Seasoning to taste

1. Heat the oil and *sauté* the sliced onion, carrot and well rinsed seaweed; cook, turning occasionally, for 5-10 minutes.

2. Add the water and cauliflower florets and simmer for 15 minutes.

3. Add the macaroni and cook for 10-15 minutes more, or until the macaroni and vegetables are just tender.

4. Pour a little of the liquid into a bowl and mix with the miso to make a smooth paste; return this to the saucepan and stir in. Let the soup stand for a few minutes without heating it further, then adjust the seasoning and serve.

LENTIL AND PASTA SOUP

4 oz (100g) brown lentils
2 pints (1.1l) vegetable stock
1 tablespoonful vegetable oil
1 onion
1 carrot
2 stalks celery
2 oz (50g) wholewheat pasta shells
1 teaspoonful yeast extract
Seasoning to taste
Parsley to garnish

1. Peel and dice the carrot; slice the onion and celery as finely as possible.

2. In a saucepan, combine the vegetable stock, oil, lentils, prepared vegetables, yeast extract and seasoning; bring to boil for 10 minutes, then cover and simmer for 45 minutes.

3. Add the pasta and stir well; add more liquid if the soup is too thick; cover and cook for 10 minutes more, or until the pasta is tender.

4. Serve piping hot, sprinkled generously with fresh chopped parsley.

ONION SOUP

1½lb (675g) onions
1oz (25g) polyunsaturated margarine
2oz (50g) plain wholemeal flour
2pts (1.1 l) water
1 teaspoonful yeast extract
1 bay leaf
2oz (50g) wholewheat spaghetti rings
4oz (100g) grated Cheddar cheese
Seasoning to taste

1. Heat the margarine in a pan until melted and gently *sauté* the peeled, sliced onions for 10 minutes, or until golden.

2. Sprinkle in the flour and cook briefly; add the water, bay leaf and seasoning, and bring to the boil.

3. Drop in the pasta, cover the pan, and simmer for 10 more minutes, by which time the pasta and onions should be tender; remove the bay leaf.

4. Serve in individual bowls with grated cheese sprinkled on top.

CLEAR WATERCRESS SOUP WITH NOODLES

2 bunches fresh watercress
4 oz (100 g) mushrooms
2 oz (50 g) bean sprouts
2 or 3 spring onions
1 tablespoonful vegetable oil
1¾ pts (965 ml) vegetable stock
2 oz (50 g) wholewheat or buckwheat noodles
Soy sauce

1. Heat the oil and fry the chopped onions for a few minutes, then add the coarsely chopped watercress and cook for a few minutes more.

2. Add the stock and bring to a fast boil before adding the sliced mushrooms and broken noodles.

3. Cook for 5-7 minutes more or until the noodles are cooked; sprinkle in the bean sprouts, turn off the heat; leave the soup to stand for a few minutes.

4. Serve flavoured with soy sauce and garnished – if liked – with extra watercress.

MEDITERRANEAN PASTA SALAD

6 oz (175 g) wholewheat macaroni
4 large tomatoes
1 large green pepper
4 spring onions
4 hard-boiled eggs
2 oz (50 g) Cheddar cheese
12 black olives
4 oz (100 g) cooked green peas
Approx. 4 tablespoonsful French salad dressing
2 teaspoonsful chopped basil
Seasoning to taste

1. Cook the macaroni for about 10 minutes, or until just tender.

2. Drain; then rinse in cold water until the pasta is cold, and drain once more.

3. In a bowl, mix together the pasta, quartered tomatoes, thinly sliced pepper, chopped onions, peas and olives.

4. Add the salad dressing, herbs, and seasoning, and toss gently.

5. Serve in a salad bowl decorated with the halved eggs, and cheese cut into small cubes.

FRUIT AND PASTA SALAD

3 oz (75 g) wholewheat spaghetti rings
2 medium bananas
2 oz (50 g) dates
2 oz (50 g) Brazil nuts
4 oz (100 g) cottage cheese
1 tablespoonful honey – optional
1 large crisp lettuce

1. Cook the spaghetti rings in boiling water; drain, then rinse in cold water.

2. In a bowl, combine the chopped bananas, dates and nuts with the spaghetti rings.

3. Arrange the washed lettuce decoratively on a serving dish, and pile the pasta, fruit and nut mixture in the centre.

CHICK PEA SALAD

8 oz (225 g) cooked chick peas
1 cucumber
1 small cooked beetroot
6 spring onions
3 oz (75 g) wholewheat macaroni

For Dressing
2 tablespoonsful cider vinegar
6 tablespoonsful vegetable or olive oil
½-1 clove garlic, crushed
Parsley to garnish

1. Drop the macaroni into boiling water and cook for 10 minutes, or until just softening; drain and rinse immediately with cold water.

2. Chop the cucumber, spring onions and beetroot into even-sized pieces.

3. Mix together the drained chick peas, macaroni and prepared vegetables.

4. Put the vinegar, oil and garlic into a screw-top jar and shake to mix thoroughly (or, better still, use a liquidizer to combine the ingredients).

5. Pour dressing to taste over the salad and leave to stand for a short while before serving garnished with the parsley. (If you prefer, you can chop the parsley fine and add it to the dressing).

CAULIFLOWER AND PASTA SALAD

6 oz (175g) wholewheat pasta shells
1 medium cauliflower
1 green pepper
4 firm tomatoes
6 tablespoonsful mayonnaise
2 oz (50g) ground nuts
Lemon juice
Seasoning to taste

1. Cook the pasta in plenty of boiling water until just tender;
   drain and rinse through with cold water; set aside.

2. Break the cauliflower into florets (these can be used raw, or
   steam them for 5 minutes to soften slightly).

3. Finely chop the green pepper, quarter the tomatoes.

4. Grind the nuts to a powder and mix into the mayonnaise,
   adding a little lemon juice and seasoning to taste.

5. In a bowl, combine the pasta, cauliflower and green pepper;
   pour on the dressing and mix gently but thoroughly.

6. Serve decorated with the tomatoes.

EGG SALAD WITH MACARONI

6 oz (175 g) wholewheat macaroni
1 ripe avocado
¼ pt (140 ml) plain yogurt
Good squeeze of lemon juice
1 teaspoonful capers – optional
4 hard-boiled eggs
Seasoning to taste
1 crisp lettuce

1. Drop the pasta into boiling water and cook for 10 minutes; drain and rinse with cold water.

2. Peel the avocado, remove the stone and cube the flesh: then mash with the yogurt (or combine in a blender until smooth).

3. Add the lemon juice and seasoning to the dressing, and – if you like a sharper taste – the finely chopped capers.

4. Mix together the pasta and dressing and arrange on a base of shredded lettuce; top with quartered eggs.

SPAGHETTI RING SLAW

4 oz (100g) wholewheat spaghetti rings
½ small white cabbage
1 medium green pepper
2 medium carrots
Chives
2 tablespoonsful mayonnaise
2 tablespoonsful soured cream
1-2 teaspoonsful caraway seeds – optional
Seasoning to taste

1. Cook the pasta until just tender; drain, and rinse well under cold running water.

2. Shred or grate the cabbage finely, and slice the pepper; peel, then grate the carrots.

3. Combine the vegetables; add the spaghetti rings.

4. Mix together the mayonnaise and soured cream so that they are thoroughly blended; add the chopped chives.

5. Pour the dressing over the mixed vegetables; season to taste; sprinkle with seeds if using them. Serve chilled.

WALDORF SALAD WITH PASTA

4 oz (100g) wholewheat pasta shells
3 medium apples
3 medium sticks celery
2 oz (50g) raisins
2 oz (50g) walnuts
2 teaspoonsful lemon juice
Approx. 4 tablespoonsful plain yogurt
Seasoning to taste
A few lettuce leaves

1. Cook the pasta in the usual way; drain, then rinse thoroughly in cold water. Set aside.

2. Core but do not peel the apples; cut into even chunks.

3. Slice the celery into small pieces.

4. Mix together all the ingredients, with seasoning to taste.

5. Chill, then serve arranged on a base of lettuce leaves.

BROAD BEAN AND MUSHROOM SALAD

8 oz (225 g) cooked broad beans
8 oz (225 g) mushrooms
2 large firm tomatoes
3 oz (75 g) wholewheat pasta shells
Vinaigrette salad dressing
Soya Smokey Snaps ('bacon' bits)

1. Wash and slice the mushrooms and mix them with the cooked, drained broad beans; quarter the tomatoes and add them to the salad.

2. Cook the pasta in boiling salted water until tender, then drain and rinse through immediately with cold water.

3. Add the pasta to the other ingredients and toss them all in the vinaigrette dressing.

4. Sprinkle with soya bacon bits and serve in an attractive dish or on a base of crisp lettuce.

LETTUCE NUT SALAD WITH GARLIC DRESSING

2 oz (50g) wholewheat spaghetti rings
1 large crisp lettuce (Webbs are ideal)
1 head of chicory
1 small curly endive
3 oz (75g) walnuts

For Dressing
2 egg yolks
2 cloves garlic, crushed
1/3 pt (190 ml) vegetable oil
1 tablespoonful lemon juice
Seasoning to taste

1. Cook the pasta in boiling water, rinse through with cold water and set aside.

2. To make the dressing, crush the garlic with the seasoning, place in a bowl and very gently add the egg yolks; blend.

3. Now add the oil drop by drop, whisking well after each one to make a thick sauce. (This can also be done using a blender if you have one.) Stir in the lemon juice.

4. Add more oil or a drop more lemon juice if the dressing is too thick.

5. Wash and shred or chop the salad greens; combine and arrange them in a bowl; sprinkle with the pasta around the edge and the chopped nuts in the centre.

6. Serve the garlic dressing separately and toss the salad at the table, just before it is eaten.

GREEN PEPPER AND PASTA SALAD

3 oz (75 g) wholewheat macaroni
3-4 green peppers
4-6 spring onions
2 oz (50 g) roasted peanuts
2 oz (50 g) Gouda cheese or similar
1 large carrot
Approx. 4 tablespoonsful mayonnaise
Seasoning to taste
½ small white cabbage to serve

1. Cook the macaroni in the usual way and rinse through
    immediately with cold water.

2. Wash and chop the onions, slice the peeled carrot; trim and
    chop two of the peppers; cube the cheese.

3. Mix them all together in a bowl with the well drained pasta,
    and just enough mayonnaise to moisten; season to taste.

4. Shred the cabbage very finely and lay it in the base of an
    attractive serving bowl; spoon the mixture over it.

5. Slice the remaining peppers crossways to make rings and
    arrange these on top of the salad, then sprinkle with the
    nuts.

COOKER-TOP RECIPES

PASTA SCRAMBLE

4 oz (100g) wholewheat pasta shells
4 eggs
2 tablespoonsful milk or cream
2 oz (50g) polyunsaturated margarine
4 oz (100g) cooked sweet corn, drained
3 large tomatoes
Seasoning to taste
Chives or parsley to garnish

1. Cook the pasta shells in boiling salted water.

2. Meanwhile, melt the margarine in a pan.

3. Beat the eggs and milk together, then pour onto the melted margarine and cook gently, stirring continually.

4. As the mixture begins to thicken, turn the heat even lower; add the sweet corn, quartered tomatoes, and drained pasta.

5. Cook for just a minute or two to heat through; season generously.

6. Serve garnished with chopped chives or parsley.

BEAN AND PASTA STEW

3 oz (75 g) wholewheat pasta shells
3 oz (75 g) well cooked haricot beans (freshly prepared, left-
    overs or tinned)
1 large carrot
1 large leek
1 large onion
1 large potato
1 tablespoonful vegetable oil
½ pt (275 ml) water
2 teaspoonsful mixed herbs
2 teaspoonsful tomato *purée*
Seasoning to taste

1. Peel and slice the carrot and onion; chop the leek into ½ in.
    sections; peel and cube the potato.

2. Heat the vegetable oil in a pan and gently *sauté* the prepared
    vegetables for a few minutes.

3. Add the water, herbs and tomato *purée;* bring to boil, then
    cover and simmer the vegetables for no more than 10
    minutes.

4. Add the beans and pasta and cook for 10 minutes longer, or
    until all the ingredients are just tender.

5. Season to taste and serve.

PASTA SHELLS WITH CREAMY CURRY SAUCE

8 oz (225 g) wholewheat pasta shells
2 oz (50 g) cashew nut pieces
4 oz (100 g) cooked peas
1 oz (25 g) polyunsaturated margarine
1 oz (25 g) plain wholemeal flour
½ pt (275 ml) milk
½-1 teaspoonful ground cumin
½-1 teaspoonful turmeric
Good pinch ground cardamom
Good pinch paprika
Seasoning to taste
Parsley to garnish

1. Cook the pasta shells in boiling water until just tender; keep warm.

2. Meanwhile, heat the margarine in a pan and add the flour; *sauté* gently for a few minutes.

3. Remove from the heat and pour in the milk, stirring continually.

4. Bring to the boil and then simmer to make a thick sauce; add the peas and sprinkle in the cumin, turmeric, cardamom and seasoning; cook for a few minutes more.

5. Mix together the cooked drained pasta, cashew nuts, and creamy curry sauce; serve immediately, topped with paprika and some coarsely chopped parsley.

SWEET AND SOUR PASTA

8 oz (225 g) wholewheat pasta shells
2 tablespoonsful vegetable oil
1 onion
1 oz (25 g) plain wholemeal flour
Approx. ¾ pt (425 ml) vegetable stock or water
1 tablespoonful cider vinegar
2 teaspoonsful thin honey
2 teaspoonsful soy sauce
Pinch of dry mustard
8 oz (225 g) cubed pineapple
Seasoning to taste
2 oz (50 g) chopped almonds
Parsley to garnish

1. Heat the oil in a large pan and gently *sauté* the chopped onion for 5 minutes.

2. Add the flour and cook until beginning to brown; stir in the vegetable stock and bring to the boil, then simmer until the sauce thickens.

3. Add the cider vinegar, honey, soy sauce, crushed pineapple, mustard and seasoning, and cook gently for a few minutes more.

4. At this stage, you can add the pasta to the sauce, cover the pan, and cook gently for 15 minutes more until the pasta is tender (you may need to add more liquid to the sauce);
   or
   Cook the pasta separately in the usual way and, when tender, drain and mix into the sauce.

5. Serve on individual plates sprinkled with nuts and parsley.

Note: This recipe is low on protein, but makes an ideal side dish with such foods as nut roast, soya meat cutlets or lentil fritters. When serving it as a side dish, you will probably only need half the quantities given here.

PASTA SHELLS WITH SESAME SAUCE

6 oz (175 g) wholewheat pasta shells
2 oz (50 g) roasted sesame seeds
6 oz (175 g) cottage or ricotta cheese
4 oz (100 g) bean sprouts
Soy sauce
Seasoning to taste

1. Grind the seeds to a powder; sieve or blend the cottage cheese to make a smooth *purée*; combine the seeds and cheese with the soy sauce and seasoning to taste; add a little hot water to make a pouring consistency.

2. Cook the pasta shells in boiling salted water until just tender; drain; mix with the bean sprouts.

3. Pour the sauce over the pasta and sprouts, stirring to make sure it is evenly distributed.

4. Serve at once; or return to the pan and heat through very gently for just a minute or two.

SEMOLINA GNOCCHI
(Fried)

4 oz (100g) wholewheat semolina
1 pt (550ml) milk
1 oz (25g) grated Parmesan cheese
1 oz (25g) polyunsaturated margarine
2 eggs
Pinch of nutmeg
Seasoning to taste
Wholemeal breadcrumbs
Vegetable oil for frying

1. Heat the milk and, when it boils, sprinkle in the semolina, stirring continually.

2. Lower the heat and cook for 3-5 minutes until the sauce thickens.

3. Away from the heat, stir in the cheese and margarine, nutmeg and seasoning.

4. Beat one of the eggs lightly and add to the mixture; continue cooking gently for just a minute longer.

5. Turn the mixture onto an oiled or wetted plate or dish.

6. When completely cold, cut into rounds with a cutter or small glass, (or shape the dough into a cylinder and slice off sections).

7. Beat the egg and season; drop the *gnocchi* into the egg and then the breadcrumbs.

8. Shallow fry until brown and crispy.

POTATO GNOCCHI

2 lb (900g) potatoes
8 oz (225g) plain wholemeal flour
½ teaspoonful baking powder
2 eggs
1 oz (25g) polyunsaturated margarine
Good pinch of nutmeg
Seasoning to taste

1. Peel, cube, and gently steam the potatoes; when cooked, drain well, then mash to a dry *purée*.

2. Add the flour, baking powder, eggs, margarine, nutmeg and seasoning, and mix to form a dough; beat until smooth.

3. On a lightly floured board, knead the dough until shiny and pliable.

4. Form the dough into rolls the shape of a finger; cut into 1 in. pieces, and shape into crescents.

5. Set aside in the cool for 15-30 minutes.

6. Fill a pan with salted water and bring to a gentle boil; drop the *gnocchi* into the water, a few at a time, and cook for 3 minutes, or until they float to the top.

7. Use a perforated spoon to remove them from the water; drain, and keep them warm whilst cooking the rest of the *gnocchi*.

8. Serve in a shallow dish with some butter or margarine, tomato sauce and/or grated cheese.

Note: Another simple and delicious sauce for potato *gnocchi* can be made by melting 2-3 oz (50-75g) grated Gorgonzola cheese with a little water, milk or cream.

SPINACH AND RICOTTA GNOCCHI

8 oz (225 g) cooked spinach, fresh or frozen
8 oz (225 g) ricotta cheese
2 eggs
4 oz (100 g) plain wholemeal flour
4 oz (100 g) grated Parmesan cheese
2 oz (50 g) polyunsaturated margarine
Pinch of nutmeg
Seasoning to taste

1. Drain and chop the spinach.

2. Put into a bowl and mix well with the ricotta cheese, half the Parmesan, nutmeg and seasoning.

3. When well blended, add the two beaten eggs.

4. Mix most of the flour into the mixture, then set aside to cool for 15-30 minutes.

5. Shape the dough into small balls; smooth the surface, and roll in the remaining flour.

6. Drop the *gnocchi* gently, a few at a time, in boiling salted water; simmer for 3-4 minutes, or until they rise to the surface.

7. Remove with a perforated spoon; drain on paper towels; keep hot whilst continuing to cook the rest of the *gnocchi* in the same way.

8. Arrange in a warmed serving dish; dot with margarine and sprinkle with the rest of the Parmesan cheese.

PASTA WITH CHICK PEA SAUCE

8 oz (225 g) wholewheat tagliatelle
4 oz (100 g) cooked chick peas
1 large onion
1 clove garlic, crushed
1 tablespoonful vegetable oil
2 tablespoonsful tahini sesame paste
Parsley to garnish
Seasoning to taste

1. Cook the pasta in the usual way until just tender.

2. Meanwhile, heat the oil and lightly *sauté* the garlic and sliced onion for 5 minutes.

3. In a blender, crush the drained chick peas with the onion to make a smooth paste (or chop coarsely if you prefer a crunchier texture to your sauce).

4. Mix with the tahini and some chopped parsley, plus a little of the water in which the chick peas were cooked, to make a sauce-like consistency.

5. Season to taste.

6. Serve the hot, drained pasta with a generous topping of the sauce, and sprinkle with more chopped parsley.

TAGLIATELLE WITH MUSHROOM YOGURT SAUCE

8 oz (225 g) wholewheat tagliatelle
2 oz (50 g) polyunsaturated margarine
½ pt (275 ml) milk
½ pt (275 ml) plain yogurt
2 oz (50 g) plain wholemeal flour
4 oz (100 g) mushrooms
4 oz (100 g) grated Parmesan cheese
Parsley and a little nutmeg
Seasoning to taste

1. Cook the tagliatelle until just tender.

2. Meanwhile, melt the margarine in a pan, then add the sliced mushrooms and *sauté* for a few minutes.

3. Sprinkle in the flour and cook for a minute or two longer.

4. Combine the milk and yogurt and stir in gradually; cook gently until the sauce is thick and creamy.

5. Add the nutmeg, some chopped parsley, and seasoning to taste.

6. Mix the drained tagliatelle with the sauce, making sure the pasta is evenly coated.

7. Serve on individual plates, sprinkled with grated Parmesan cheese.

BEAN SPROUTS TAGLIATELLE

8 oz (225 g) wholewheat tagliatelle
1 oz (25 g) polyunsaturated margarine
1 medium onion
1 medium carrot
1 clove of garlic, crushed
1 small apple
4 tablespoonsful tomato *purée*
½ oz (15 g) plain wholemeal flour
½ pt (275 ml) water or vegetable stock
2-3 oz (50-75 g) fresh bean sprouts
Seasoning to taste

1. To make a tomato sauce, finely chop or grate the peeled onion and carrot, and *sauté* with the garlic in the melted margarine.

2. After a few minutes, add the grated apple and cook for a little longer.

3. Blend the flour with the water or stock; stir in the tomato *purée*; add to the pan and season to taste.

4. Bring the sauce to the boil, then leave to simmer for 10 minutes, stirring occasionally.

5. Meanwhile, cook the tagliatelle in boiling water, then drain.

6. Add the bean sprouts to the tomato sauce and cook gently for 2 minutes longer to heat through.

7. Serve the tagliatelle topped with the tomato and bean sprouts sauce.

CLASSIC PESTO SAUCE FOR PASTA

8 oz (225 g) tagliatelle or pasta of your choice
1 oz (25 g) pine nuts
2 teaspoonsful fresh basil leaves or 1 teaspoonful dried
    basil
2 oz (50 g) grated Parmesan cheese
1 clove garlic, crushed
3-4 tablespoonsful olive oil
Seasoning to taste

1. In a mortar, pound the basil and garlic together with a little coarse sea salt and black pepper.

2. Add the nuts, pounding them to a smooth paste.

3. Add the finely grated cheese and mix thoroughly to make a thick *purée*.

4. Gradually trickle in the oil, stirring continually, until you have a creamy smooth sauce.

5. Cook the tagliatelle in boiling water for 10 minutes, drain and serve immediately with the *pesto*.

Note: If you cannot get pine nuts, walnuts can be used instead.

BLENDER PESTO SAUCE WITH SPINACH

8 oz (225 g) fresh spinach, washed and dried
4 oz (100 g) fresh basil leaves
4-6 tablespoonsful olive oil
1 tablespoonful grated Parmesan cheese
1 tablespoonful pine nuts
1 clove garlic

1. Trim the coarse stems from the spinach and basil leaves.

2. Put all the ingredients together into the blender and whizz until they make a thick, green sauce.

3. Chill until needed.

TAGLIATELLE WITH CELERY AND EGG

10 oz (275 g) wholewheat tagliatelle
1 oz (25 g) polyunsaturated margarine
2 tablespoonsful vegetable oil
1 onion
4 sticks celery
4 tomatoes
2 tablespoonsful tomato *purée*
1 oz (25 g) plain wholemeal flour
4 hard-boiled eggs
Seasoning to taste

1. Cook the tagliatelle in boiling salted water until tender; drain and set aside.

2. Melt the margarine in a saucepan together with the oil; lightly *sauté* the sliced onion for 5 minutes; add the finely chopped celery and cook for 5 minutes more, stirring frequently.

3. Sprinkle in the flour and cook until beginning to brown; add the skinned, chopped tomatoes and tomato *purée* and cook gently until you have a thick sauce. (If it seems too dry add a little more *purée* and/or water.)

4. Mix the pasta into the celery sauce and return to a gentle heat for a minute to heat through; season to taste.

5. Serve the tagliatelle with the coarsely chopped eggs scattered over the top.

ARTICHOKE HEARTS AND PASTA

8 oz (225 g) wholewheat tagliatelle
6 globe artichokes
3 oz (75 g) cooked peas
2 tablespoonsful vegetable oil
1 onion
3 tomatoes
1-2 teaspoonsful capers, chopped small
4 oz (100 g) grated Parmesan cheese

1. Wash the artichokes, peel off the coarse outer leaves and trim the stalks; slice horizontally.

2. Heat the oil and fry the chopped onion gently for a few minutes, then add the artichokes and cook together for 5 minutes more.

3. Stir in the chopped tomatoes and capers and simmer for 30 minutes, or until the vegetables are tender.

4. Add the drained peas and pasta; mix well; season to taste.

5. Heat through for one minute only, then serve with the cheese sprinkled on top.

MUSHROOM RICE RAVIOLI

8 oz (225 g) basic pasta dough
Approx. 4 oz (100 g) cooked brown rice
6 oz (175 g) mushrooms
2 oz (50 g) Cheddar cheese
Parsley
1 large onion
4 large ripe tomatoes
2 tablespoonsful vegetable oil
Seasoning to taste

1. Roll out the pasta dough as thinly as possible; cut into small squares; set half aside, and arrange the rest on a flat surface.

2. Make a tomato sauce: fry the sliced onion in a tablespoonful of oil, then add the mashed tomatoes and seasoning, and cook on a medium heat until a *purée* is formed.

3. Heat the rest of the oil and lightly *sauté* the chopped mushrooms.

4. Combine equal amounts of rice with the mushrooms (too much rice will make the ravioli heavy).

5. Add the grated cheese, a generous amount of chopped parsley, and seasoning.

6. Spoon a little of the mixture onto each dough square.

7. Lay the rest of the pasta squares over the fillings; press down dampened edges gently but firmly.

8. Drop the ravioli, a few at a time, into a large pan of boiling water; cook for 5-10 minutes, or until they rise to the surface.

9. Remove the ravioli with a perforated spoon; drain, then put them in a warm spot whilst cooking the rest.

10. Serve the ravioli topped with the tomato sauce.

RAVIOLI WITH SPINACH

8 oz (225 g) basic pasta dough
6 oz (175 g) cooked spinach
6 oz (175 g) cream, curd, cottage or ricotta cheese
3 oz (75 g) grated Parmesan cheese
2 eggs
Good pinch of nutmeg
Seasoning to taste

1. Roll out the pasta dough, as thinly as possible; cut into small squares; set half aside, and arrange the rest on a flat surface to be filled.

2. Drain the spinach, put it into a bowl and mix well with the cream cheese and 1 oz (25 g) of the Parmesan cheese.

3. Add the beaten eggs; season to taste.

4. Use a teaspoon to drop a small amount of the spinach cheese mixture in the centre of the squares of dough.

5. Cover each one with another square of dough; press the edges together lightly but firmly, being careful not to trap air in the 'envelope'. (Edges will stick better if dampened with water or a little beaten egg first.)

6. Bring salted water to the boil in a large pan; drop in the ravioli a few at a time, and cook gently for 5-10 minutes, or until they rise to the surface.

7. Take out of the water with a perforated spoon; drain well; arrange in a warmed serving dish.

8. Serve the ravioli sprinkled with the remaining Parmesan cheese.

NUT SAVOURY FILLED RAVIOLI

8 oz (225 g) basic pasta dough
4 oz (100 g) Brazil nuts, ground or finely chopped
3 oz (75 g) wholemeal breadcrumbs
1 oz (25 g) wheat germ
1 tablespoonful vegetable oil
1 leek
1 teaspoonful sage, or to taste
Seasoning to taste
Yeast extract – optional
1 oz (25 g) melted polyunsaturated margarine

1. Roll out the pasta dough; cut into small squares; arrange half of them on a flat surface and put the rest aside.

2. Fry the cleaned and finely chopped leek in the oil until soft; remove the pan from the heat and stir in the nuts, crumbs, wheat germ, sage and seasoning.

3. Flavour the mixture with a little yeast extract if liked, then use a wooden spoon to mash all the ingredients and make a paste.

4. Drop a small amount of the mixture in the centre of each of the squares of dough.

5. Cover each one with another square of dough; dampen the edges and press firmly together.

6. Bring salted water to the boil in a large pan and drop in the ravioli, a few at a time; cook gently for 5-10 minutes, or until they rise to the surface.

7. Use a perforated spoon to remove the ravioli from the water; drain and serve with a little melted margarine trickled over them.

DEEP-FRIED RAVIOLI

8 oz (225g) basic pasta dough
1 oz (25g) polyunsaturated margarine
1 oz (25g) plain wholemeal flour
¼ pt (140ml) milk
4 oz (100g) grated Cheddar cheese
Vegetable oil for frying
Seasoning to taste
Parsley to garnish

1. Roll out the dough as thinly as possible; cut into small squares; arrange half on a flat surface and put the rest to one side.

2. Make a very thick white sauce: melt the margarine in a pan, add and gently *sauté* the flour until lightly browned; stir in the milk and continue cooking until the sauce thickens.

3. Add the cheese and seasoning; if the sauce is still too thin, thicken with some more cheese and/or a few wholemeal breadcrumbs.

4. Put a spoonful of the filling onto each square of dough and cover with a second square; dampen the edges and press down to form a well-sealed packet.

5. Drop the ravioli, a few at a time, into the hot vegetable oil, and cook steadily until crisp and golden (this should only take a few minutes).

6. Drain the ravioli on absorbent paper towels before serving, garnished with fresh chopped parsley.

MACARONI MEXICANA

4 oz (100g) wholewheat macaroni
4 oz (100g) well cooked kidney beans
1 large onion
1 large green pepper
3 medium tomatoes
1 clove garlic, crushed
2 tablespoonsful vegetable oil
1-2 teaspoonsful chilli powder or to taste
1 teaspoonful paprika
Seasoning to taste

1. Cook the macaroni in plenty of boiling water; when just tender, drain and set aside.

2. Heat the oil in a pan; add the coarsely chopped onion and pepper with the crushed garlic, and *sauté* for 10 minutes.

3. Add the drained beans, chopped tomatoes, spices and seasoning, and simmer for 5-10 minutes more to heat through. (If the mixture is too dry, add a few spoonsful of the water in which the beans were cooked.)

4. When ready, mix the drained macaroni gently into the bean sauce; adjust seasoning, and serve.

QUICK MACARONI CHEESE

8 oz (225 g) wholewheat macaroni
6 oz (175 g) curd cheese
2 oz (50 g) Cheddar cheese
2 tablespoonsful chopped tarragon or dill – optional
2 tablespoonsful wholemeal breadcrumbs
Seasoning to taste

1. Cook the macaroni in boiling water for 10 minutes, drain well.

2. Stir in the curd cheese until it melts to make a creamy sauce; add herbs and seasoning.

3. Transfer to a flat heatproof dish; top with grated Cheddar cheese and breadcrumbs.

4. Put under the grill for 2 minutes to brown.

MACARONI BURGERS

4 oz (100g) wholewheat macaroni
2 oz (50g) polyunsaturated margarine
2 oz (50g) plain wholemeal flour
½ pt (275 ml) milk
4 oz (100g) Cheddar cheese
2 oz (50g) cooked peas or green beans
1 teaspoonful rosemary
Approx. 2 oz (50g) wheat germ
Seasoning to taste
Extra wheat germ or wholemeal breadcrumbs
Vegetable oil for frying

1. Cook the macaroni until just tender; drain, and rinse through thoroughly with cold water; set aside.

2. Melt the margarine in a pan and lightly *sauté* the flour.

3. Remove from the heat; pour on the milk; return to the heat, and continue cooking and stirring until the sauce thickens.

4. Add the grated cheese, coarsely chopped peas or beans, crumbled rosemary; season generously.

5. Mix the sauce with the drained macaroni and leave to cool.

6. Shape the mixture into burgers – if it is too soft, add a little wheat germ or breadcrumbs.

7. Coat each one with wheat germ and shallow- or deep-fry until crisp and golden.

MACARONI BUBBLE AND SQUEAK

1 medium cabbage
1 large onion
6 oz (175 g) wholewheat macaroni
2 oz (50 g) polyunsaturated margarine
2 oz (50 g) grated Cheddar cheese
Seasoning to taste

1. Cook the macaroni in boiling water until just tender; drain and set aside.

2. Shred the cabbage coarsely and steam for 5-10 minutes.

3. Melt the margarine in a saucepan and add the onion; *sauté* until just beginning to soften.

4. Add the drained cabbage and macaroni and continue frying, stirring frequently, until everything begins to colour.

5. Season, then press the mixture down to a flat round pancake; transfer to a heatproof plate and cover with the grated cheese.

6. Put under the grill for a few minutes until the cheese melts; serve at once, cut into wedges.

Note: As with the usual Bubble and Squeak, this is an ideal way to use left-overs!

FENNEL SAUCE WITH PASTA

8 oz (225 g) wholewheat macaroni
1 small fennel bulb
1 oz (25 g) polyunsaturated margarine
1 oz (25 g) plain wholemeal flour
½ pt (275 ml) milk
Good pinch of nutmeg
1 small lemon
1 egg yolk
A little cream
Seasoning to taste

1. Cook the macaroni in the usual way; when tender, drain and set aside.

2. Melt the margarine and gently *sauté* the flour until it begins to brown; stir in the milk and bring to the boil, then continue simmering until a sauce forms.

3. Add the finely chopped fennel, a good squeeze of lemon juice and some of the rind, grated finely; season.

4. In another bowl, mix together the egg yolk and 2 or 3 spoonsful of cream; then gradually pour this into the slightly cooled sauce, whisking continually.

5. Pour at once over the drained pasta; stir to make sure the sauce is evenly distributed, and serve. Some of the feathery fennel leaves make an attractive and unusual garnish.

PARSLEY EGG MACARONI

8 oz (225 g) wholewheat macaroni
1 oz (25 g) plain wholemeal flour
1 tablespoonful vegetable oil
¾ pt (425 ml) milk
Juice and grated rind of 1 lemon
3 hard-boiled eggs
3 tablespoonsful fresh chopped parsley
Seasoning to taste

1. Cook the macaroni in boiling salted water until just tender.

2. Meanwhile, heat the oil in a saucepan and *sauté* the flour for a few minutes; stir in the milk and bring to the boil, then simmer to make a sauce.

3. Remove the pan from the heat and add the lemon and rind, parsley, chopped eggs and seasoning; mix well.

4. Combine with the macaroni and re-heat gently for just a few minutes before serving.

Note: Some wholemeal breadcrumbs and/or a little grated cheese can be sprinkled on top, and the macaroni dish put under the grill for a few minutes if you prefer.

MACARONI AND VEGETABLE STEW

4 oz (100g) wholewheat macaroni
2 oz (50g) polyunsaturated margarine
1 large leek
1 parsnip
1 onion
1 potato
1 carrot
½ pt (275 ml) vegetable stock
Soy sauce
1-2 teaspoonsful mixed herbs
Seasoning to taste
Watercress to garnish

1. Peel and cube the parsnip, potato and carrot; slice the onion and leek.

2. Melt the margarine and gently *sauté* the vegetables for a few minutes; add the stock; season with soy sauce, herbs, sea salt and freshly ground black pepper.

3. Simmer until the vegetables are cooked but still hold their shape.

4. Meanwhile, cook the macaroni in boiling water.

5. Combine the drained macaroni with the vegetables and stock, and heat for 2 minutes; serve garnished with watercress.

PASTA WITH MUSHROOM GOULASH

6 oz (175 g) wholewheat spaghetti or noodles
1 oz (25 g) polyunsaturated margarine
1 onion
1 green pepper
8 oz (225 g) mushrooms
1-2 tablespoonsful paprika, or to taste
2 tomatoes
1 teaspoonful dill
$1/3$ pt (190 ml) plain yogurt or soured cream
1 oz (25 g) plain wholemeal flour
Seasoning to taste
Parsley to garnish

1. Cook the pasta in plenty of boiling salted water until just tender; drain and set aside.

2. Meanwhile, melt the margarine in a saucepan and gently fry the sliced onion and pepper for 5-10 minutes, or until soft.

3. Add the washed and chopped mushrooms, and cook for a few minutes more, stirring every now and again.

4. Sprinkle in the paprika and cook briefly, then add the chopped tomatoes with just enough water to cover; add the dill and seasoning.

5. Stir the ingredients, then cover the pan and simmer for 5 minutes.

6. Mix together the yogurt and flour and stir into the goulash; cook for a few minutes more over a very gentle heat, still stirring.

7. Serve the pasta with the goulash poured over the top; garnish with fresh chopped parsley.

BROCCOLI SPAGHETTI

8 oz (225 g) wholewheat spaghetti
8 oz (225 g) fresh broccoli
1 large onion
½-1 clove garlic
1 oz (25 g) polyunsaturated margarine
1 tablespoonful vegetable oil
2 oz (50 g) pine nuts
Parmesan cheese – optional
Seasoning to taste

1. Bring a saucepan of water to the boil and add sea salt; add the spaghetti and cook for 10 minutes or until just tender.

2. Meanwhile, steam the broccoli and then drain well; chop as small as possible.

3. Heat the margarine and oil together; *sauté* the finely sliced onion and garlic until the onion begins to soften.

4. Add the broccoli and nuts; season well; continue cooking over a gentle heat, stirring occasionally.

5. When the broccoli and onion mixture is thick and sauce-like, remove from the heat.

6. Serve the spaghetti with the sauce poured over it; Parmesan cheese can be sprinkled on top if liked.

CHINESE-STYLE SPAGHETTI

8 oz (225 g) buckwheat spaghetti
4 oz (100 g) tofu (bean curd)
4 oz (100 g) mushrooms
1 medium green pepper
2 medium carrots
1 bunch watercress
2 tablespoonsful vegetable oil
Soy sauce
Seasoning to taste

1. Cook the spaghetti in boiling water for 10 minutes.

2. Heat the oil in a frying pan and add the cubed tofu; cook, stirring, until the tofu is lightly browned.

3. Peel the carrots, then slice lengthwise into thin strips; slice the mushrooms and pepper; wash and cut tough stems off the watercress.

4. Add the vegetables to the frying pan and cook over a moderate heat until tender but still crisp; sprinkle with soy sauce and season to taste.

5. Drain the spaghetti and arrange on a serving dish or individual plates; top with the tofu vegetable mixture and serve with more soy sauce if required.

PEANUTS AND PASTA

8 oz (225 g) wholewheat spaghetti
4 tablespoonsful smooth peanut butter
Approx. ¼ pt (140 ml) milk
Good pinch of chilli powder
Parsley to garnish
2 oz (50 g) roasted peanuts
Seasoning to taste

1. Cook the pasta and keep it warm.

2. In a pan, heat together the peanut butter, milk, chilli powder and seasoning; stir constantly until all the ingredients are well blended and heated through.

3. Adjust the milk, if necessary, to give the sauce a pouring consistency.

4. Drain the spaghetti. Arrange on serving dish, and pour the sauce over it.

5. Coarsely chop the parsley and peanuts and scatter on top.

SPAGHETTI 'BOLOGNESE'

8 oz (225 g) wholewheat spaghetti
6 oz (175 g) brown or green lentils, soaked overnight
1 oz (25 g) polyunsaturated margarine
1 tablespoonful vegetable oil
1 clove garlic, crushed
1 large onion
1 large green pepper
4 large ripe tomatoes or 3 tablespoonsful tomato *purée*
4 oz (100 g) mushrooms
1-2 teaspoonsful oregano
Seasoning to taste

1. Cook the lentils in boiling water until almost tender.

2. Heat the margarine and oil together in a large saucepan; fry the crushed garlic, sliced onion and pepper for several minutes over a low heat.

3. Add the chopped mushrooms and cook for a minute or two longer.

4. Stir in the lentils, chopped tomatoes or *purée*, oregano and seasoning.

5. Cover the pan and simmer gently for 15 minutes, or until cooked. (If using fresh tomatoes, the sauce may seem dry, in which case, add a little of the water in which the lentils were cooked, or tap water.)

6. Whilst the sauce is cooking, prepare the spaghetti in the usual way.

7. Drain the spaghetti, arrange on a serving dish or individual plates, and cover with the 'bolognese' sauce.

PASTA PILAF

10 oz (275 g) wholewheat spaghetti or spaghetti rings
2 oz (25 g) polyunsaturated margarine
1 large onion
2 oz (50 g) currants
2 oz (50 g) cooked peas
4 oz (100 g) pine nuts or cashew pieces
3 large tomatoes
½-1 teaspoonful ground coriander
½-1 teaspoonful ground cardamom
½-1 teaspoonful turmeric
Seasoning to taste

1. Cook the pasta in boiling water until just tender, then drain.
    (If using spaghetti, break it into small pieces first.)

2. Melt the margarine in a pan and gently *sauté* the chopped
    onion together with the spices for a few minutes.

3. Mix in the drained pasta, currants, peas, nuts and coarsely
    chopped tomatoes; stir so that all the ingredients are well
    combined; heat through for a few minutes only.

4. Season to taste, and serve hot.

CLIVE BIRCH

SPAGHETTI WITH GARLIC YOGURT

8 oz (225 g) wholewheat spaghetti
2 medium courgettes
1 oz (25 g) polyunsaturated margarine
2 cloves garlic, crushed
½ pt (275 ml) plain yogurt
Seasoning to taste

1. Cook the spaghetti in the usual way.

2. Meanwhile, top and tail the courgettes, then cut into fine slivers.

3. Melt the margarine in a pan; add the courgettes and *sauté* gently, stirring continually, until just turning brown.

4. Remove the courgettes and set aside in a warm spot.

5. Add the garlic to the pan and cook a minute or so longer.

6. Mix the contents of pan with the yogurt; add seasoning.

7. Stir the courgette slivers into the cooked, drained spaghetti; top with the garlic yogurt sauce.

PASTA OMELETTE

6 oz (175 g) wholewheat noodles
2 oz (50 g) polyunsaturated margarine
1 medium onion
4 eggs
2 oz (50 g) bean sprouts
Seasoning to taste
Watercress to garnish

1. Cook the noodles in boiling water, until just tender; drain well.

2. Melt the margarine in another pan; *sauté* the chopped onion for 5 minutes.

3. Add the bean sprouts and drained noodles; cook for a few minutes more.

4. Beat the eggs; season well; pour into the pan evenly.

5. Continue cooking until almost set, then carefully turn the omelette; cook until browned on both sides and completely set. (This can also be done by putting the omelette under the grill.)

6. Serve cut into slices, and garnished with watercress.

BUCKWHEAT NOODLES WITH MISO-TAHINI SAUCE

8 oz (225g) buckwheat noodles
1 large onion
1 tablespoonful vegetable oil
1 teaspoonful miso
2 tablespoonsful tahini sesame paste
Approx. $^1/_3$ pt (190ml) water
1 oz (25g) plain wholemeal flour

1. Cook the noodles in the usual way.

2. Meanwhile, heat the oil and gently *sauté* the sliced onion until just tender.

3. Sprinkle in the flour and cook briefly.

4. Remove the pan from the heat and add the water, then bring to boil, stirring continually.

5. As the sauce begins to thicken add the miso and tahini, and continue cooking until they have dissolved and blended completely.

6. If the sauce is too thick, add a little more water.

7. Serve the miso-tahini sauce over the drained noodles.

CLIVE BIRCH

NOODLES WITH WALNUT SAUCE

8 oz (225 g) wholewheat noodles
2 oz (50 g) walnuts
1 oz (25 g) fine wholemeal breadcrumbs
2 oz (50 g) polyunsaturated margarine
2 tablespoonsful vegetable oil
2 tablespoonsful creamy milk
Parsley to garnish
Seasoning to taste

1. Remove the skins from the walnuts if preferred.

2. Pound or grind the nuts to make a paste; add the finely chopped parsley and seasoning and mix well.

3. Use a wooden spoon to mix in the margarine, oil and crumbs; continue blending until you have a thick, creamy sauce.

4. Stir in the milk and adjust the seasoning. (If the sauce is too thick, add oil or cream to adjust the consistency.)

5. Cook the noodles in boiling water until tender; drain and serve with the walnut sauce, and a garnish of parsley.

SESAME NOODLES WITH CABBAGE

10 oz (275 g) wholewheat noodles
1 small white cabbage
2 medium onions
4 oz (100g) polyunsaturated margarine
2 oz (50g) sesame seeds
2 tablespoonsful tahini sesame paste
Seasoning to taste

1. Cook the noodles in plenty of water, then set aside.

2. Meanwhile, *sauté* the peeled, sliced onions in the melted margarine until transparent.

3. Finely shred the cabbage and add to the pan, cooking gently until tender.

4. Stir in the drained noodles and combine thoroughly.

5. Add the tahini and seeds; season to taste; serve hot.

SOYA SPAGHETTI

8 oz (225 g) wholewheat spaghetti
4 oz (100 g) soya grits
½ pt (275 ml) vegetable stock
1-2 teaspoonsful yeast extract
½-1 clove garlic, crushed
1 onion
1 tablespoonful vegetable oil
1-2 teaspoonsful oregano
4 tablespoonsful tomato *purée*
1 oz (25 g) polyunsaturated margarine
Seasoning to taste
Parsley to garnish

1. Soak the grits for a few hours or overnight in the vegetable stock, then bring to the boil for 10 minutes and simmer until the grits are soft.

2. Cook the spaghetti in the usual way.

3. Heat the oil and gently *sauté* the sliced onion with the garlic until soft but not browned.

4. Add the grits with whatever stock is left; stir in the *purée*, yeast extract, herbs and seasoning; simmer for 5-10 minutes.

5. Add a little more liquid to the grits if necessary to make a sauce; stir in the margarine until melted.

6. Arrange the spaghetti on a serving dish and pour on the sauce; garnish with fresh parsley.

SPINACH NOODLE RING

For Ring
8 oz (225 g) wholewheat noodles
¼ pt (140 ml) milk
3 oz (75 g) Cheddar cheese
2 eggs, separated
Seasoning to taste

For Filling
1 lb (450 g) spinach
2 oz (50 g) polyunsaturated margarine
Pinch of raw cane sugar
Pinch of grated nutmeg

1. Cook the noodles in boiling water; drain and chop coarsely.

2. Mix the noodles with the egg yolks and milk; add the grated cheese and season.

3. Add the whisked egg whites and pour mixture into a greased ring mould.

4. Bake in the oven at 325°F/170°C (Gas Mark 3) for 50 minutes to an hour, or until set.

5. Wash the spinach and shred; steam until cooked, then drain and chop finely.

6. Add the margarine, sugar and nutmeg to the spinach and mix thoroughly.

7. Turn the noodle ring onto a serving plate and fill the centre with the spinach mixture; serve at once.

Note: Any vegetable mixture can be used in the centre of this ring. Try a ratatouille made with aubergine, tomatoes, onions and courgettes; or cabbage with walnuts; brussels sprouts with chestnuts also go well. Serve alone, or with a tomato or cheese sauce.

HUMMUS WITH PASTA

8 oz (225 g) wholewheat noodles
2 tablespoonsful vegetable oil
1 onion
4 tomatoes
1-2 teaspoonsful oregano
4-6 tablespoonsful hummus*
Seasoning to taste
2 tablespoonsful cooked chick peas – optional

1. Cook the noodles in boiling salted water until just tender.

2. Heat the oil and *sauté* the sliced onion for a few minutes,
    then add the coarsely chopped tomatoes and cook for a few
    minutes more.

3. Season the mixture, add the herbs and enough water to just
    cover; simmer for 15 minutes.

4. Stir the hummus into the tomato sauce until it has blended
    in completely, making the sauce creamy and golden; adjust
    the seasoning.

5. Serve the pasta with the sauce poured over it; garnish with
    coarsely chopped chick peas and parsley.

*To make hummus, grind some cooked chick peas to a paste
and stir in tahini to taste; add a squeeze of lemon juice, garlic salt
and/or seasoning, a trickle of vegetable oil, and enough of the
water in which the chick peas were cooked to make the
consistency you require. Hummus can also be served as a dip
with salad vegetables, a sauce for hot vegetables, a spread in
sandwiches, or as an accompaniment to deep-fried falafels – just
adjust the consistency and seasoning to suit.

PEAS, PASTA AND CURRY CREAM SAUCE

6 oz (175 g) wholewheat noodles
6 oz (175 g) peas
1 oz (25 g) polyunsaturated margarine
1 oz (25 g) wholemeal flour
½ pt (275 ml) creamy milk or milk with 2 tablespoonsful
   skimmed milk powder added
1 teaspoonful turmeric
1 teaspoonful ground cumin
½ teaspoonful ground cardamom
2 oz (50 g) peanuts
Seasoning to taste
Pinch of paprika
Parsley to garnish

1. Cook the peas in boiling water; drain and set aside.

2. Melt the margarine in a saucepan and add the flour and spices; *sauté* for a few minutes until the flour begins to brown; pour in the milk and bring to the boil, then simmer.

3. Continue cooking and stirring until the sauce thickens.

4. Meanwhile, cook the pasta in boiling salted water until just tender.

5. Add the peas to the curry cream sauce, season, and heat through for a few minutes before stirring into the drained noodles; add the cashews.

6. Serve garnished with paprika and parsley.

Note: This is a delicate tasting sauce, and although the quantities of the spices can be increased slightly, too much will change its character completely. If you like a stronger curry flavour, use a standard sauce made the way you like, add the peas and nuts, and serve with the noodles.

ORIENTAL NOODLES

6 oz (175 g) wholewheat noodles
2 tablespoonsful vegetable oil
½ clove garlic, crushed
2 oz (50 g) hydrated soya 'meat' slices
¾ pt (425 ml) hot vegetable stock
½ small white cabbage
2 oz (50 g) bean sprouts
Good pinch of ginger
Soy sauce
Seasoning to taste

1. In a large saucepan heat the oil and gently *sauté* the crushed garlic for a minute.

2. Cut the soya 'meat' into strips and add to the pan; *sauté* for 5 minutes, turning frequently.

3. Add the stock to the pan together with the shredded cabbage, ginger, soy sauce, seasoning, and the noodles.

4. Bring to the boil, then cook over a medium heat until the cabbage and noodles are tender, and much of the liquid has been absorbed.

5. Stir in the bean sprouts and serve at once.

Note: If there is still a good deal of liquid left, you can either drain some of it off, or mix a tablespoonful of arrowroot with cold water and add this slowly to the saucepan, then cook until the sauce thickens. Adjust the seasoning. An omelette cut into strips can be arranged over the noodles for an even more filling dish.

TAGLIATELLE WITH TOFU TOMATO SAUCE

10 oz (275 g) wholewheat tagliatelle
1 lb (450 g) tomatoes
1 large onion
2 sticks celery
½-1 clove garlic
2 tablespoonsful vegetable oil
Approx. ¼ pt (140 ml) vegetable stock or water
12 oz (350 g) tofu
Seasoning to taste
Chives to garnish

1. Cook the pasta in plenty of boiling water and keep warm.

2. Heat the oil in a saucepan and *sauté* the finely chopped onion and celery sticks for a few minutes; add the garlic and the skinned, chopped tomatoes and cook a little longer.

3. Drain any excess liquid from the tofu then mash it into the ingredients in the pan – the more you break it up, the smoother your sauce will be.

4. Add a very small amount of stock, cover the pan, and simmer the sauce until it is thick; add more water if necessary during cooking process.

5. Season the tofu tomato sauce to taste and serve poured over the drained tagliatelle; sprinkle with chives.

KASHA AND PASTA

8 oz (225 g) wholewheat pasta shells
4 oz (100 g) kasha (roasted buckwheat)
½ pt (275 ml) water
1 red pepper
1 large onion
10 black olives
Capers
2 oz (50 g) polyunsaturated margarine
1 small carton soured cream
Seasoning to taste

1. Add the kasha to the water, bring to the boil, then simmer until just tender; keep warm.

2. At the same time, cook the pasta in a large pan of boiling water.

3. Melt the margarine and gently cook the sliced onion, pepper, halved olives and capers for about 10 minutes, stirring frequently.

4. Stir the soured cream into the vegetables and heat through briefly; season.

5. Combine the drained kasha and pasta and serve topped with the sauce.

WINTER VEGETABLES PASTA

8 oz (225 g) wholewheat macaroni
8 oz (225 g) parsnips
8 oz (225 g) carrots
8 oz (225 g) turnips
2 tablespoonsful vegetable oil
Approx. ½ pt (275 ml) vegetable stock
4 oz (100 g) peas
1 teaspoonful basil
4 oz (100 g) Lancashire cheese
Seasoning to taste

1. Peel and cube the root vegetables; heat the oil and *sauté* them briefly, turning frequently.

2. Pour in the stock, add the herbs, bring to the boil then cover and simmer for 20-30 minutes, or until tender.

3. Meanwhile, cook the pasta in boiling water; drain well.

4. Mix together the vegetables and pasta and transfer to a shallow heat-proof dish – most of the liquid will probably have been absorbed, but if not, drain off the excess first.

5. Season to taste; sprinkle with the grated cheese, and pop under the grill for a minute or two. Serve as the main dish, or make smaller portions and serve as a vegetable with such savouries as fritters, nut loaves, etc.

BAKED DISHES

BLUE CHEESE LASAGNE

6 oz (175 g) wholewheat lasagne
4 oz (100 g) Danish blue cheese ⎫
4 oz (100 g) Cheddar cheese ⎬ grated and mixed
1½ pts (825 ml) milk
2 oz (50 g) polyunsaturated margarine
2 oz (50 g) plain wholemeal flour
½ small carton soured cream
Seasoning to taste

1. Cook the lasagne in boiling water until just tender; rinse in cold water and set aside.

2. Melt the margarine in a pan; stir in the flour and cook gently until beginning to brown; add the milk and continue stirring until the sauce thickens.

3. Remove from the heat and blend in most of the grated cheese with the soured cream; season to taste, (you will need little, if any, sea salt).

4. Layer the prepared lasagne with the sauce in a shallow ovenproof dish, finishing with sauce. (If necessary, add a little more milk to make the sauce easier to pour.)

5. Sprinkle with the remaining cheese.

6. Bake at 400°F/200°C (Gas Mark 6) for 30 minutes.

LASAGNE WITH RED PEPPERS

6 oz (175 g) wholewheat lasagne
2 medium onions
2 medium red peppers
3 medium tomatoes
10 black olives
2 tablespoonsful vegetable oil
1 teaspoonful basil
2 oz (50 g) walnut pieces
¾ pt (425 ml) plain yogurt
2 eggs
2 oz (50 g) Cheddar cheese
Seasoning to taste

1. Cook the lasagne; drain, then rinse thoroughly in cold water.

2. Heat the vegetable oil and gently *sauté* the sliced onions and peppers until they start to soften.

3. Add the walnuts and cook for a few minutes more.

4. Chop the tomatoes and add to the pan with the basil and seasoning; simmer for 5 minutes, stirring often.

5. Stone and halve the olives; stir into the vegetables.

6. Layer half the lasagne in a greased heatproof dish; top with the vegetable nut mixture; cover with the rest of the lasagne.

7. Beat the eggs lightly; add to the yogurt; season well.

8. Pour the sauce over the lasagne, tipping the dish so that it runs down between the ingredients.

9. Sprinkle with the grated cheese.

10. Bake at 400°F/200°C (Gas Mark 6) for 30-40 minutes, or until set.

VEGETABLE LASAGNE WITH TAHINI

4 oz (100g) wholewheat lasagne
2 tablespoonsful vegetable oil
2 medium onions
2 sticks celery
2 medium carrots
½ small cauliflower, broken into florets
4 oz (100g) cooked green peas
2 oz (50g) plain wholemeal flour
2 tablespoonsful tahini, or to taste
Seasoning to taste
Parsley to garnish

1. Cook the lasagne in boiling water; when just tender, remove at once from the heat and rinse through with cold water. Set aside.

2. Heat the oil in a large pan; gently *sauté* the peeled and chopped onions and carrots with the sliced celery, stirring occasionally.

3. When the vegetables are beginning to colour, add the flour and cook for a few minutes, then stir in the cauliflower florets, and enough water to cover.

4. Simmer until all the ingredients are cooked but still firm; add the drained peas carefully, and tahini to flavour the sauce.

5. In a shallow ovenproof dish layer the lasagne with the vegetables, finishing with lasagne and then a few spoonsful of sauce (or use a little more tahini with water).

6. Bake at 400°F/200°C (Gas Mark 6) for 20-30 minutes. Serve garnished with plenty of fresh parsley.

GREEK-STYLE LASAGNE

6 oz (175 g) wholewheat lasagne
8 oz (225 g) soya 'minced meat'
1 medium onion
4 medium tomatoes
2 medium aubergines
2 tablespoonsful vegetable oil
1 clove garlic, crushed
Parsley
1-2 teaspoonsful oregano
1 small carton soured cream or plain yogurt
2 oz (50 g) grated Parmesan cheese
Seasoning to taste

1. Cook the lasagne in the usual way; after rinsing in cold water, set aside.

2. Cut the aubergine into ½ in. slices – arrange on a plate; sprinkle with sea salt and leave to drain for 30 minutes.

3. Hydrate the soya 'meat' according to instructions.

4. Heat the oil in a pan; add the sliced onion and garlic and cook gently for 5 minutes.

5. Rinse and dry the aubergine, chop into cubes and add to the pan; cook for 5 minutes more, stirring frequently.

6. Add the chopped tomatoes, herbs and seasoning.

7. Spoon in the soya 'meat' with just a little of the liquid in which it was cooked; cover the pan and simmer all the ingredients for about 10 minutes.

8. Layer a third of the lasagne in the base of a greased, heatproof dish; top with half the 'meat' mixture; add a few spoonsful of soured cream.

9. Repeat this pattern once more.

10. Top with the rest of the lasagne, then the soured cream; sprinkle with the grated cheese; season.

11. Bake, uncovered, at 375°F/190°C (Gas Mark 5) for 30 minutes, or until the top is golden.

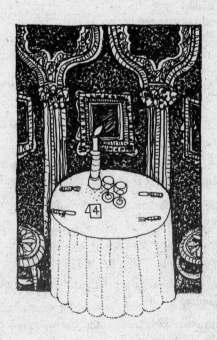

ADUKI BEAN AND VEGETABLE LASAGNE

4 oz (100 g) wholewheat lasagne
4 oz (100 g) cooked aduki beans
2 medium onions
2 medium leeks
2 medium carrots
1 tablespoonful vegetable oil
1 oz (25 g) polyunsaturated margarine
1 oz (25 g) plain wholemeal flour
½ pt (275 ml) milk
3 oz (75 g) Cheddar cheese
1-2 teaspoonsful sage
Seasoning to taste

1. Cook the lasagne for 15 minutes in boiling water; drain, then rinse in cold water. Set aside.

2. Heat the oil in a pan and gently *sauté* the sliced onions, leeks and carrots for 10 minutes.

3. Add a sprinkling of water, the sage and seasoning; cover the pan and simmer until the vegetables are tender.

4. Meanwhile, melt the margarine in another pan; sprinkle in the flour and *sauté* briefly.

5. Add the milk; bring to boil, then cook over a low heat, stirring continually, until the sauce thickens.

6. Grease a shallow heatproof dish and cover the bottom with half the lasagne.

7. Mix together the vegetables and drained beans, and distribute evenly in the dish.

8. Pour on half the white sauce (if too thick, add a little extra milk or water); cover with the remaining lasagne.

9. Add the rest of the sauce, spreading it to make an even top-
    ping; sprinkle with grated Cheddar cheese.

10. Bake at 400°F/200°C (Gas Mark 6) for 30 minutes.

BOSTON BAKED BEANS LASAGNE

4 oz (100 g) wholewheat lasagne

For Beans
8 oz (225 g) haricot beans, soaked overnight
1 oz (25 g) polyunsaturated margarine
2 onions
8 oz (225 g) cooking tomatoes
3 tablespoonsful tomato *purée*
2 teaspoonsful muscovado raw cane sugar
2 teaspoonsful molasses
1 teaspoonful dry mustard
Good pinch of ground cinnamon and cloves
Seasoning to taste
3 oz (75 g) Cheddar cheese – optional

1. Drain the beans; add fresh water; bring to the boil for 10 minutes then simmer for an hour.

2. Heat the margarine and *sauté* the skinned and chopped tomatoes and onions until just softening; add the tomato *purée*, sugar, molasses, mustard, spices and seasoning.

3. Drain the beans and add about ½ pt (275 ml) of the liquid to the sauce; bring to the boil, stirring, then tip the beans back into the saucepan and blend well.

4. Transfer the mixture to an ovenproof dish, cover, and bake at 300°F/150°C (Gas Mark 2) for about 4 hours, or until the beans are tender. (Stir the mixture occasionally and add more liquid if necessary.)

5. Meanwhile, cook the pasta in boiling water for 10-15 minutes; drain, and rinse with cold water.

6. Place a layer of lasagne in the bottom of a shallow ovenproof dish, cover with some of the beans and sauce; repeat this until all the ingredients have been used; top with grated cheese (or finish with a generous layer of sauce).

7. Bake at 400°F/200°C (Gas Mark 6) for 20-30 minutes.

Note: In an emergency, you can use tinned baked beans in this dish – they will taste more authentic if you simmer them briefly with some onion and molasses before making up the lasagne.

CANNELLONI WITH 'MINCED MEAT'

8 oz (225 g) basic pasta dough
6 oz (175 g) cooked spinach
3 oz (75 g) soya 'minced meat' (dry weight)
1 clove garlic, crushed
1 medium onion
4 tablespoonsful vegetable oil
4 oz (100 g) grated Parmesan cheese
1 oz (25 g) plain wholemeal flour
½ pt (275 ml) milk
1 oz (25 g) polyunsaturated margarine
Seasoning to taste

1. Roll out the pasta dough as thinly as possible; cut into 8 rectangles approximately 5 in. x 4 in. in size.

2. Cook the pasta in boiling salted water, stirring occasionally, for 5-10 minutes, or until tender but still firm.

3. Remove from the pan with a perforated spoon; drain and pat dry; spread on a plate and leave covered.

4. Hydrate the soya 'minced meat' according to the instructions on the packet.

5. Heat 2 tablespoonsful of the oil in a pan; add the sliced onion and garlic; fry gently until soft.

6. Add the drained 'meat' and simmer until cooked, (you may need to sprinkle with some water or stock).

7. Stir in the finely chopped spinach, seasoning, and 2 oz (50 g) of the grated cheese; mix thoroughly.

8. Divide the filling between the rectangles of dough; roll up carefully; place neatly in a greased heatproof dish, with the joint side down.

9. Make the white sauce; heat the rest of the oil in a pan, *sauté* the flour, then pour in the milk and bring to a boil before simmering to thicken the sauce.

10. Pour the sauce over the cannelloni; top with the rest of the grated cheese; dot with the margarine.

11. Bake at 400°F/200°C (Gas Mark 6) for 20 minutes.

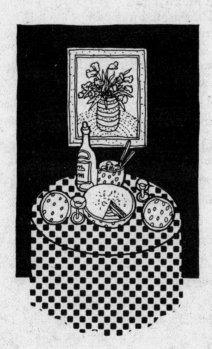

WALNUT CANNELLONI

8 oz (225g) basic pasta dough
1 large onion
2 large courgettes
2 tablespoonsful vegetable oil
4 oz (100g) wholemeal breadcrumbs, soaked in water
1 large egg
2 oz (50g) chopped walnuts
Parsley
1 small carton plain yogurt
2 oz (50g) grated Parmesan cheese
Seasoning to taste

1. Roll out the pasta dough as thinly as possible; cut into 8 rectangles approximately 5 in. x 4 in. in size.

2. Cook the pasta in boiling salted water, stirring occasionally, for 5-10 minutes, until tender but still firm.

3. Remove from the pan with a perforated spoon; drain and pat dry; spread on a plate and leave covered.

4. Heat the oil in another pan and lightly *sauté* the finely chopped onion and courgettes for 5 minutes.

5. Drain, then squeeze the breadcrumbs and add them to the pan with the parsley, chopped nuts and seasoning; cook until golden.

6. Cool slightly, then add the egg to the mixture, blending thoroughly.

7. Divide the filling between the rectangles of dough; roll them up and place close together, joint side down, in a greased heatproof dish.

8. Cover with the plain yogurt, sprinkle with cheese; bake at 400°F/200°C (Gas Mark 6) for about 30 minutes.

CABBAGE AND SOUR CREAM CANNELLONI

8 oz (225 g) basic pasta dough
1 large onion
½ small white cabbage
2 oz (50g) pumpkin or sunflower seeds
2 oz (50g) polyunsaturated margarine
1 small carton soured cream
2 oz (50g) grated Parmesan cheese
Seasoning to taste

1. Roll out the pasta dough and, when it is as thin as you can make it, cut into 8 rectangles approximately 5 in. x 4 in. in size.

2. Add carefully to the boiling salted water and cook, stirring occasionally, for 5-10 minutes, until tender but still firm.

3. Remove from the pan with a perforated spoon; drain and pat dry; spread on a plate and leave covered.

4. Heat the margarine in a pan and gently cook the finely sliced onion for 5 minutes; add the grated cabbage and continue cooking over a low heat, stirring occasionally, until soft.

5. Mix in the seeds, season, then divide the filling between the pasta rectangles.

6. Roll them carefully and place, with the join on the bottom, side by side in a greased ovenproof dish.

7. Stir together the soured cream and grated cheese, season to taste, then pour over the pasta rolls.

8. Bake at 400°F/200°C (Gas Mark 6) for 20 minutes.

Note: If desired, you can also mix a little soured cream and/or cheese with the cabbage before filling the cannelloni.

LENTIL CANNELLONI

8 oz (225 g) basic pasta dough
8 oz (225 g) small red lentils
3 tablespoonsful vegetable oil
2 onions
½-1 clove garlic, crushed
1 bay leaf
1 teaspoonful chopped parsley
1 teaspoonful thyme
4 tablespoonsful bean sprouts – optional
Approx. ¾ pt (425 ml) vegetable stock
4-6 tablespoonsful tomato *purée* or home-made tomato
  sauce
Seasoning to taste

1. Roll out the pasta to a thin sheet; cut into 8 rectangles
   approximately 5 in. x 4 in. in size.

2. Add the pasta to boiling salted water and cook for 5-10
   minutes, or until just tender.

3. Remove carefully with a perforated spoon, then pat dry; lay
   on a plate and leave covered.

4. Heat the oil in a pan; add the crushed garlic and finely sliced
   onions; cook gently until softening.

5. Add the lentils and cook for just a few minutes before
   pouring in the stock; sprinkle with the herbs and seasoning,
   and bring to the boil for 10 minutes.

6. Lower the heat, cover the pan, and simmer until all the
   liquid has been absorbed, which should take 30-40 minutes.
   (Add a tiny amount of liquid if necessary.)

7. Remove the bay leaf, then use a wooden spoon to mash the
   lentils to a thick *purée*; leave to cool slightly.

8. Mix in the bean sprouts, if using them.

9. Divide the mixture between the rectangles of dough, and roll each one carefully.

10. Place them neatly, side by side, in a shallow greased ovenproof dish, preferably with the joint facing downwards.

11. Cover generously with tomato *purée* or sauce, season, and bake at 400°F/200°C (Gas Mark 6) for 20-30 minutes.

'SAUSAGE ROLLS'

8 oz (225 g) basic pasta dough or wholewheat lasagne
5 oz (150 g) nut and cereal mix or soya 'sausage' mix (from
   a health food shop)
2 tablespoonsful vegetable oil
1 onion
1 green pepper
1 lb (450 g) cooking tomatoes
2 tablespoonsful tomato *purée*
1-2 teaspoonsful oregano
Seasoning to taste
2 oz (50 g) cottage cheese mixed with 1 oz (25 g) grated
Parmesan cheese – optional

1. Roll out the pasta dough as thinly as you can; cut into strips about 2 in.-3 in. x 5 in. in size; cook the pasta in plenty of boiling salted water for about 10 minutes, or until just cooked.

2. Drain the pasta, rinse in cold water and set aside.

3. Make up the filling according to the packet instructions.

4. If using lasagne strips, cut into half so that you have small rectangles similar in size to those described above, (exact size is not that important).

5. Fill each rectangle with some of the mixture and roll up into a sausage shape; place them neatly side by side in a greased ovenproof dish.

6. Make the sauce: heat the oil and gently *sauté* the sliced onion and pepper for 5 minutes, then add the chopped tomatoes, *purée* and seasoning with about ½ pt (275 ml) water.

7. Bring to the boil, then simmer the sauce until thick.

8. Pour this mixture over the 'sausage' rolls; spread with cheese if liked, and bake at 400°F/200°C (Gas Mark 6) for 20-30 minutes.

Note: You can also make this dish with ready-cooked soya 'meat' sausages, bought tinned from most health food shops. And try it with a bechamel or cheese sauce instead of tomato sauce for a change.

CANNELLONI WITH EGG FILLING

8 oz (225 g) basic pasta dough
4 hard-boiled eggs
4 medium carrots
1 oz (25 g) polyunsaturated margarine
1 oz (25 g) plain wholemeal flour
¾ pt (425 ml) milk
4 oz (100 g) Cheddar cheese
3 tablespoonsful wholemeal breadcrumbs
Seasoning to taste

1. Roll out the pasta as thinly as possible; cut into 8 rectangles approximately 5 in. x 4 in. in size.

2. Bring a large pan of salted water to the boil; add the pasta and cook for 5-10 minutes, or until just tender.

3. Use a perforated spoon to remove the pasta from the pan; drain and pat dry, then arrange on a plate and leave covered.

4. Chop the peeled carrots into small pieces and steam until cooked but still crisp; drain, and mix with the finely chopped eggs.

5. Make a white sauce by melting the margarine in a pan, gently *sautéeing* the flour for a few minutes, then pouring in most of the milk and stirring until the mixture thickens.

6. Season the sauce, then add about half of it to the egg and carrot, blending well.

7. Adjust the seasoning, then use this mixture to fill the rectangles of pasta; roll them up and lay close together, join facing downwards, in a greased ovenproof dish.

8. Add the rest of the milk to the sauce, if necessary, to make a pouring consistency, then spread it over the cannelloni.

9. Sprinkle the dish with the grated cheese and breadcrumbs, and bake at 400°F/200°C (Gas Mark 6) for 20-30 minutes.

PASTA SOUFFLÉ

4 oz (100g) wholewheat spaghetti rings
1 oz (25g) polyunsaturated margarine
½ oz (15g) plain wholemeal flour
¼ pt (140ml) milk
3 oz (75g) Cheddar cheese
3 eggs, separated
Pinch of cayenne pepper
Seasoning to taste

1. Cook the spaghetti rings in the usual way; drain well and set aside.

2. Melt the margarine in a saucepan, add the flour, and cook for a few minutes.

3. Remove from the heat and stir in the milk; then continue cooking until sauce boils, stirring continually.

4. Simmer briefly, then set aside to cool slightly.

5. Stir in the grated cheese; add the pasta; season and blend well.

6. Add the egg yolks, one at a time.

7. Whisk the egg whites until stiff and carefully fold them into the pasta sauce.

8. Grease a medium-sized *soufflé* or casserole dish, and pour in the mixture.

9. Bake at 375°F/190°C (Gas Mark 5) for 25-30 minutes, or until well risen and set. Serve at once.

BEAN AND BRUSSELS HOT-POT

4 oz (100g) wholewheat spaghetti rings
3 oz (75g) well cooked butter beans
2 tablespoonsful vegetable oil
2 onions
1-2 garlic cloves, crushed
10 oz (275g) small brussels sprouts
4 tomatoes
Approx. ½ pt (275 ml) vegetable stock
1 teaspoonful yeast extract, or to taste
Seasoning to taste

1. Heat the oil in a pan and *sauté* the sliced onions and garlic until lightly browned.

2. Add the cleaned brussels sprouts with the stock, yeast extract, seasoning, coarsely chopped tomatoes and drained beans.

3. Turn the mixture into a casserole and cook, covered, in the oven, at 350°F/180°C (Gas Mark 4) for 10 minutes.

4. Stir in the pasta, adjust the liquid if necessary (remember the pasta will absorb quite a bit).

5. Return to the oven at the same temperature and continue cooking for 15-20 minutes, or until the pasta is just tender.

SPAGHETTI BAKE

8 oz (225 g) wholewheat spaghetti
1 lb (450 g) fresh spinach
8 oz (225 g) curd or cream cheese
A little milk
1 oz (25 g) polyunsaturated margarine
3 oz (75 g) wholemeal breadcrumbs
Seasoning to taste

1. Cook the spaghetti in boiling salted water until barely tender; drain and set aside.

2. Steam the washed spinach; when cooked, drain and chop finely.

3. Soften the curd cheese and combine with the spinach; add a little milk if the mixture is very firm; season generously.

4. Toss the spaghetti with the creamed spinach until thoroughly combined; pile the mixture into an ovenproof dish; spread as evenly as possible.

5. In a saucepan, melt the margarine over a low heat; add the breadcrumbs and fry them briefly; sprinkle them over the spaghetti.

6. Bake at 350°F/180°C (Gas Mark 4) for 20 minutes, or until the top is crisp and golden.

BAKED AUBERGINE WITH PASTA

2 medium aubergines
2 onions
3 tomatoes
½-1 clove garlic, crushed
1 tablespoonful vegetable oil
1 oz (25 g) polyunsaturated margarine
3 oz (75 g) wholewheat pasta shells
2 oz (50 g) grated Cheddar cheese
2 oz (50 g) walnuts
Seasoning to taste

1. Cook the pasta in boiling salted water until just tender; drain and set aside.

2. Wash the aubergines and boil them for a few minutes; cool slightly; cut carefully in half lengthways and scoop out the flesh. (Keep the skins.)

3. Heat the oil and margarine together in a pan, and *sauté* the sliced onions with the garlic until just beginning to colour.

4. Add the coarsely chopped aubergine flesh and tomatoes, and continue cooking gently, stirring occasionally, for 10 more minutes.

5. Remove the pan from the heat and mix the pasta with the vegetables; season to taste; divide the mixture between the four shell-halves.

6. Arrange them on a lightly greased baking sheet; sprinkle with grated cheese and chopped walnut pieces.

7. Bake at 350°F/180°C (Gas Mark 4) for 20 minutes, or until cooked.

BAKED MACARONI WITH CAULIFLOWER

6 oz (175 g) wholewheat macaroni
1 medium cauliflower
1 tablespoonful vegetable oil
1 oz (25 g) plain wholemeal flour
½ pt (275 ml) milk or stock from cauliflower with 2
    tablespoonsful skimmed milk powder
4 oz (100 g) Edam cheese
2 tablespoonsful soya 'bacon' or wholemeal breadcrumbs
Good pinch of nutmeg
Seasoning to taste

1. Cook the macaroni in the usual way, then drain well.

2. Break the cauliflower into florets and steam, or cook in the minimum amount of water, until just tender.

3. Heat the oil in another pan, add the flour and cook for a few minutes.

4. Remove from the heat and stir in the milk, then bring to the boil and simmer until the sauce thickens.

5. Add the grated cheese and the seasoning; combine with the cauliflower and macaroni.

6. Pour into a casserole, smooth the top, and sprinkle with the soya 'bacon' or breadcrumbs; add the nutmeg.

7. Bake at 350°F/180°C (Gas Mark 4) for 15 minutes, or until heated through.

BRAZIL NUT BAKE

4 oz (100g) wholewheat macaroni
4 oz (100g) Brazil nuts, ground finely
4 oz (100g) Cheddar cheese
1 large egg
1 medium courgette
1-2 teaspoonsful mixed herbs
Seasoning to taste

1. Cook the macaroni until just tender, then drain well and chop coarsely.

2. Grate the cheese and the washed courgette (leave the skin on).

3. In a bowl, mix together the macaroni, ground Brazil nuts, grated cheese and courgette, herbs and seasoning.

4. Lightly beat the egg and add to the other ingredients.

5. Grease a shallow dish, pour in the mixture, and bake at 325°F/170°C (Gas Mark 3) for 30-40 minutes, or until set.

SESAME-TOPPED MACARONI

8 oz (225 g) wholewheat macaroni
1 onion
2 green peppers
2 tablespoonsful vegetable oil
1-2 teaspoonsful mixed herbs
Approx. ¼ pt (140 ml) plain yogurt or soured cream
4 oz (100 g) sesame seeds, ground to a powder
1 oz (25 g) polyunsaturated margarine
Seasoning to taste

1. Cook the macaroni in boiling salted water; when just tender, remove from the cooker and drain.

2. In a saucepan, heat the oil and *sauté* the sliced onion and peppers until softened; add the herbs and seasoning.

3. Stir together the pasta, vegetable mixture and enough yogurt to make a creamy sauce.

4. Turn the mixture into an ovenproof dish.

5. Melt the margarine and mix with the powdered seeds; spread this over the top of the pasta and vegetables.

6. Bake at 350°F/180°C (Gas Mark 4) for about 15 minutes.

CREAMY NOODLES BAKE

8 oz (225 g) wholewheat noodles
8 oz (225 g) cottage cheese
2 oz (50 g) polyunsaturated margarine
1 medium onion
1 medium red pepper
2 large eggs
Chives to garnish
Seasoning to taste

1. Cook the noodles in the usual way; drain well.

2. Sieve, blend or mash the cottage cheese to make a smooth sauce.

3. Mix the cheese sauce and noodles; stir in the margarine until it melts.

4. Finely chop the peeled onion and the pepper, and add to the mixture with the beaten eggs and seasoning.

5. Lightly grease a flan dish, pour in the noodle mixture, and bake at 350°F/180°C (Gas Mark 4) for 30 minutes, or until set.

6. Sprinkle with chives before serving.

PASTA-STUFFED PEPPERS

4 large peppers
4 oz (100g) wholewheat noodles
1 medium onion
2 medium sticks celery
4 oz (100g) ground nuts
2 oz (50g) Edam cheese
1 large egg
1-2 teaspoonsful mixed herbs
Soy sauce
1 tablespoonful vegetable oil
Seasoning to taste

1. Break the noodles into pieces and cook in boiling water until just tender; drain, then set aside.

2. Peel and chop the onion as finely as possible; slice the celery sticks finely; grate the cheese.

3. In a bowl, combine the noodles, chopped onion and celery, nuts and cheese.

4. Beat the egg lightly, then add to the other ingredients with the herbs, seasoning, and a sprinkling of soy sauce.

5. Wash the peppers and slice off the tops; remove the core and pips.

6. Stand the peppers close together in a small greased heat-proof dish; spoon in the pasta stuffing.

7. Replace the pepper tops and brush lightly with a little vegetable oil; bake at 400°F/200°C (Gas Mark 6) for 30-40 minutes, or until the peppers and stuffing are cooked.

GOLDEN VEGETABLE NOODLES

10 oz (275 g) wholewheat noodles
1 large parsnip
1 large carrot
1 large potato
4 oz (100 g) cooked sweet corn
Approx. ¾ pt (425 ml) milk
1 teaspoonful dill
1 oz (25 g) polyunsaturated margarine
Seasoning to taste
2 oz (50 g) grated Cheddar cheese
2 tomatoes

1. Cook the noodles in boiling salted water until just tender; drain and set aside.

2. Peel and finely chop the parsnip, carrot and potato.

3. Heat the margarine in a saucepan; when melted, add the prepared vegetables and cook gently for 10 minutes, stirring frequently.

4. Pour in the milk, add the herbs and seasoning; cover the pan and simmer for 20 minutes.

5. Cool the vegetables slightly, then put them into a blender to make a thick, golden *purée*; adjust the liquid if necessary.

6. Layer half the noodles in a shallow ovenproof dish; cover with half the vegetable *purée*; sprinkle with half the cooked, drained sweet corn. Repeat this to use up all the ingredients.

7. Cover the top of the dish with grated cheese; decorate with slices of tomato.

8. Bake at 350°F/180°C (Gas Mark 4) for 20 minutes.

EGG AND ONION LASAGNE

6 oz (175g) wholewheat lasagne
1½lb (675g) onions
2 oz (50g) polyunsaturated margarine
1 teaspoonful caraway seeds – optional
1 oz (25g) plain wholemeal flour
4 hard-boiled eggs
4 oz (100g) Parmesan cheese
Seasoning to taste

1. Cook the lasagne in boiling water and, when tender, rinse in cold water; drain and set aside.

2. Melt the margarine and *sauté* the crushed caraway seeds for a minute, then add the thickly sliced onions and cook gently for 5-10 minutes, stirring frequently.

3. Cover the pan and leave to cook over a low heat for 10 minutes more – if the pan seems dry add a spoonful of water.

4. Stir in the flour, cook briefly, add the milk and continue cooking and stirring until the onions are coated in a white sauce; add extra milk if it is too thick, and season well.

5. Layer the ingredients in an ovenproof dish in the following order: lasagne, sliced eggs, onions in sauce, then repeat.

6. Finish with the grated cheese, and bake at 400°F/200°C (Gas Mark 6) for 20-30 minutes.

AUBERGINE YOGURT LAYER

8 oz (225g) wholewheat macaroni
2 aubergines
3 tablespoonsful vegetable oil
2 oz (50g) plain wholemeal flour
1 clove garlic, crushed
1 large onion
8 oz (225g) tomatoes
2 oz (50g) polyunsaturated margarine
2 oz (50g) plain wholemeal flour
¾pt (415ml) milk
½pt (275ml) yogurt
3 oz (75g) wholemeal breadcrumbs
Parsley
Seasoning to taste

1. Slice the aubergines; arrange them on a plate and sprinkle with salt; leave for 30 minutes.

2. Rinse and dry the aubergine slices and dip into the seasoned flour; fry gently in 2 tablespoonsful of the oil until tender on the inside, crisp and brown on the outside; drain on paper towels.

3. Heat the rest of the oil and *sauté* the garlic and finely chopped onion; add the peeled, crushed tomatoes and cook to make a thick *purée*.

4. In another pan, melt the margarine and sprinkle in the flour; *sauté* briefly; add the milk and stir whilst cooking until the sauce thickens; remove from the heat, season, and add the yogurt.

5. Cook the macaroni in boiling water then drain well.

6. Arrange half the macaroni in the base of an ovenproof dish; spread with half the tomato *purée*; cover with half of the aubergine slices; top with half the yogurt sauce.

7. Repeat this to use up the rest of the ingredients, and top with a mixture of the crumbs, chopped parsley and seasoning.

8. Bake this dish at 350°F/180°C (Gas Mark 4) for about 30 minutes.

Note: You can speed up the time spent preparing this dish by using ready-made tomato *purée* or sauce, or simply use slices of fresh tomatoes; and the yogurt sauce can be replaced by plain yogurt.

PASTA HOT-POT

4 oz (100g) wholewheat macaroni
4 oz (100g) hydrated soya 'meat' chunks
8 oz (225g) carrots
2 onions
8 oz (225g) peas
4 oz (100g) mushrooms
4 tomatoes
1-2 teaspoonsful mixed herbs
Approx. 1 pt (550ml) vegetable stock
Seasoning to taste

1. In a large saucepan, combine the drained 'meat' chunks, sliced carrots, onions and peas; pour the stock over them and bring to the boil.

2. Transfer the ingredients to a casserole, cover, and cook in the oven at 325°F/170°C (Gas Mark 3) for about 30 minutes.

3. Add the seasoning and herbs, sliced mushrooms and quartered tomatoes; stir in the macaroni having first cooked it for 10 minutes in boiling water.

4. Leave the casserole uncovered and continue cooking for 15-30 minutes more, or until all the ingredients are cooked.

PASTA DESSERTS

VERMICELLI PEACH CONDÉ

3 oz (75 g) wholewheat vermicelli
1 pt (550 ml) milk
2 oz (50 g) light muscovado raw cane sugar
Pure vanilla essence to taste
2 large fresh peaches
1/3 pt (190 ml) pure orange juice
Barely 1 oz (25 g) arrowroot
2 oz (50 g) desiccated or flaked coconut to garnish

1. Simmer the vermicelli in the milk for 10-20 minutes, or until the pasta is tender and most of the milk has been absorbed.

2. Add the sugar and essence; spoon the slightly cooled mixture into 4 dessert dishes or glasses.

3. Mix a little of the fruit juice with the arrowroot, then add to the rest and heat gently in a pan, stirring continually, to make a sauce.

4. Halve and stone the peaches; place one half cut-side down on the top of each dish.

5. Pour the fruit sauce over the fruit and pasta carefully and leave to set in the cool; serve sprinkled with coconut.

DRIED FRUIT BAKE

4 oz (100g) wholewheat macaroni
1 pt (550ml) milk
2 oz (50g) dried apricots, soaked overnight
2 oz (50g) dried prunes, soaked overnight
2 oz (50g) raisins
½ teaspoonful mixed spice, or to taste
1-2 teaspoonsful grated orange or lemon peel
Cream to serve – optional

1. Cook the macaroni in the milk for 15-20 minutes, or until tender.

2. Wash the dried fruit, pat dry, and chop the apricots and prunes into smaller pieces.

3. Combine all the ingredients and transfer to an ovenproof dish.

4. Bake at 350°F/180°C (Gas Mark 4) for 20 minutes.

5. Serve hot or cold, with cream if liked.

Note: With so much dried fruit, this dish should be sweet enough without additional sugar. If, however, you have an especially sweet tooth, you could mix the spice with a little raw cane sugar and sprinkle it over the top before baking.

PASTA CARAMEL

4 oz (100g) wholewheat macaroni
1 pt (550ml) milk
2 oz (50g) light muscovado raw cane sugar
2 tablespoonsful water
Knob of polyunsaturated margarine

1. Put the sugar into a saucepan with the water; heat gently, stirring continually, until the sugar dissolves; cook a little longer to form a brown caramel mixture.

2. Add the milk and heat gently.

3. Add the macaroni and the margarine; continue cooking until the pasta is tender and most of the liquid has been absorbed.

4. If you prefer, this mixture can be transferred to an ovenproof dish and baked at 300°F/150°C (Gas Mark 2) for 30 minutes.

NOODLES WITH FRUIT SAUCE

3 oz (75 g) wholewheat noodles
3 cooking apples
8 oz (225 g) blackcurrants
2 tablespoonsful pure honey or raw sugar blackcurrant jam
Good squeeze of lemon juice
Plain yogurt to serve

1. Cook the noodles in boiling water for 5-10 minutes or until
    tender.

2. Peel, core and slice the apples; wash the blackcurrants; cook
    the fruit together in a heavy pan with enough water to cover.

3. When soft, mash or sieve the fruit to make a *purée*; sweeten
    with honey or jam; add the lemon juice.

4. Serve the pasta with the hot fruit sauce poured over it and
    well mixed in. A few whole blackcurrants could be reserved
    and sprinkled on top. Serve the yogurt separately.

Note: This can be eaten as you would eat a savoury noodle dish,
with a spoon and fork, or break the pasta into small pieces
before cooking so that it can be easily picked up in a spoon.

PEAR, DATE AND PASTA COMPOTE

4 dessert pears
4 oz (100g) whole dates
4 oz (100g) wholewheat spaghetti rings
1 lemon
3 oz (75g) light muscovado raw cane sugar
¾ pt (425 ml) water
Vanilla raw sugar ice cream to serve

1. In a saucepan, combine the water, sugar, lemon juice and some of the grated rind; bring to the boil and continue boiling for about 15 minutes.

2. Peel, core and halve the pears.

3. Simmer the pears in the syrup until just tender; add the washed dates and cook for a few minutes longer.

4. Meanwhile, cook the pasta rings in boiling water for 10 minutes; drain and add to the fruit and syrup; mix well.

5. Serve hot; or leave to get cold, during which time the pasta will absorb some of the syrup flavour. Ice cream goes well with this compote.

MACARONI AND GOOSEBERRY CRUNCH

3 oz (75 g) wholewheat macaroni
1 pt (550 ml) milk
3 oz (75 g) light muscovado raw cane sugar
1 egg
8 oz (225 g) gooseberries
4 oz (100 g) muesli
1 oz (25 g) polyunsaturated margarine

1. Cook the cleaned gooseberries with 2 oz (50 g) of sugar and a little water.

2. Simmer the macaroni in the milk for 20-30 minutes or until soft. Sweeten with the rest of the sugar.

3. Remove from the heat, cool slightly; add the beaten egg, and continue cooking over a low heat, stirring continually, for 5 minutes more or until thick and creamy.

4. Spoon the macaroni into a shallow ovenproof dish, smooth the top.

5. Cover with the softened gooseberries (strain first if very liquid).

6. Melt the margarine in a pan and toss in the muesli; cook gently for just a minute; sprinkle this mixture over the prepared dish.

7. Put under the grill briefly to make the topping crisp; serve hot.

STUFFED APPLES

4 large apples
4 oz (100g) raw sugar mincemeat
2 oz (50g) wholewheat spaghetti rings
2 oz (50g) chopped roasted hazelnuts
½ oz (15g) polyunsaturated margarine
1 tablespoonful pure honey
Squeeze of lemon juice
1 small carton plain yogurt – optional
¼ pt (140ml) single cream – optional

1. Cook the pasta in boiling water until tender; drain, then set aside.

2. Wash, dry, and remove the centre cores from the apples; make a slit around the skins so that the apples do not burst in the oven.

3. In a bowl, mix together the pasta, mincemeat, nuts and margarine. Stuff the apples with this mixture.

4. Arrange the apples side-by-side in an ovenproof dish; mix the honey with the lemon juice and trickle over the top of the apples.

5. Bake at 350°F/180°C (Gas Mark 4) for about 40 minutes, or until the apples are cooked.

6. Serve hot or cold.

Note: Yogurt and single cream whipped lightly together, then chilled, make a fresh contrast to the sweetness of this dish.

INDIAN-STYLE VERMICELLI

4 oz (100g) wholewheat vermicelli
2 oz (50g) polyunsaturated margarine
½ teaspoonful cardamom powder, or to taste
1 pt (550ml) milk
3 oz (75g) demerara raw cane sugar
1 oz (25g) raisins
1-2 oz (25-50g) pistachio nuts

1. Heat half the margarine and gently fry the raisins and coarsely chopped nuts for 5 minutes, stirring continually.

2. Transfer them to another bowl; add the rest of the margarine, and when melted, add the spice and cook briefly.

3. Add the vermicelli, broken into pieces, to the pan and fry gently, stirring frequently, until it begins to change colour.

4. Pour in the milk, add the sugar and bring to boil; simmer until the pasta is soft and the mixture thick and creamy.

5. Spoon into individual glasses or dessert dishes and sprinkle generously with the nuts and raisins.

6. Serve hot or cold.

NOODLE PUDDING

8 oz (225 g) wholewheat noodles
2 eggs, separated
2 apples
2 oz (50 g) chopped dried apricots
2 oz (50 g) walnuts
1 teaspoonful mixed spice
2 tablespoonsful pure honey
Pinch of sea salt

1. Cook the noodles in boiling water until just tender; drain
    well.

2. Core, and chop the apples coarsely.

3. Beat the egg yolks lightly; add the apple, apricot pieces,
    chopped nuts, spice, honey and salt.

4. Stir in the drained pasta, making sure all the ingredients are
    well mixed together.

5. Whisk the egg whites until just stiff enough to hold a shape;
    fold into the noodles.

6. Lightly grease an ovenproof dish and turn the mixture into
    it; bake at 350°F/180°C (Gas Mark 4) for 30 minutes, or
    until firm. Serve piping hot.

MELON WITH PASTA SHELLS

1 large melon
10 black grapes
10 white grapes
10 cherries or strawberries
2 bananas
2 oz (50g) wholewheat pasta shells
3 tablespoonsful raw sugar apricot jam
Squeeze of lemon juice
Whipped cream – optional

1. Cook the pasta shells in boiling water until tender; drain and rinse immediately with cold water.

2. Cut the top off the melon; remove the seeds and most of the flesh.

3. Make a sauce by heating the sieved jam, lemon juice, and some water in a saucepan, stirring frequently.

4. Wash and dry the grapes and cherries; peel and chop the bananas; chop the melon flesh that was removed earlier.

5. Mix all the fruit and the drained pasta into the sauce, making sure all the ingredients are coated; if necessary, make up some extra sauce.

6. Pile back carefully into the melon shell; pour on any extra sauce.

7. Serve, if liked, with whipping cream.

Note: Any fruit can be used in this dessert, including dried varieties. Nuts can be added, and the sauce can be made of pure honey and lemon juice instead of jam. Alternatively, try mixing the fruit with a honey and yogurt sauce, and sprinkling with coconut.

EGG CUSTARD SURPRISES

4 oz (100g) wholewheat spaghetti rings
1 pt (550ml) milk
2 or 3 eggs
1 oz (25g) raw cane sugar
2 oz (50g) candied peel
2 oz (50g) raisins
Grated nutmeg

1. Cook the spaghetti rings in water (or milk) until just tender; drain well and divide between 4 small *soufflé* or ovenproof dishes.

2. Sprinkle each one with some of the raisins and chopped peel. ·

3. In a bowl, whisk together the eggs and warmed milk; add the sugar; pour over the pasta and fruit, preferably through a strainer; sprinkle with nutmeg

4. Stand the dishes in a tin of hot water and bake at 325°F/170°C (Gas Mark 3) for 1 hour, or until set.

APRICOT FLAN

For Pastry
5 oz (150g) plain wholemeal flour
3 oz (75g) polyunsaturated margarine
1 egg

For Filling
6 apricots
3 oz (75g) almonds, preferably roasted
1 teaspoonful pure vanilla essence
½ pt (275 ml) plain yogurt
6 oz (175g) cream cheese
1 tablespoonful honey

3 oz (75g) wholewheat spaghetti rings

1. Put the flour into a bowl; rub in the fat with the finger-tips; use the beaten egg to bind to make a firm dough.

2. Knead the dough lightly then roll it out to line an 8 in. flan dish; bake blind at 400°F/200°C (Gas Mark 6) for about 30 minutes, or until cooked.

3. In a bowl, blend together the cream cheese, yogurt, honey and vanilla essence.

4. Cook the pasta in water until tender; drain well.

5. Distribute the pasta across the base of the cooled flan; halve and stone the apricots and arrange them attractively on top, cut-side down.

6. Spoon over the yogurt mixture and smooth the top; sprinkle with the chopped nuts; put the flan in a cool spot until the filling sets.

SWEET APPLE LASAGNE

6 oz (175g) wholewheat lasagne
2 lb (900g) cooking apples
4 oz (100g) raw cane sugar, or to taste
2 teaspoonsful ground cinnamon, or to taste
1-2 tablespoonsful lemon or orange juice
2 oz (50g) walnuts, coarsely chopped
2 oz (50g) wholemeal breadcrumbs
½ oz (15g) polyunsaturated margarine

1. Cook the lasagne in boiling water, then rinse in cold water and set aside.

2. Core and slice the apples and put into a pan with the spice, lemon juice, sugar, and enough water to cover; simmer until soft.

3. Place a layer of the lasagne in an ovenproof dish; cover with half the apple *purée*; use the rest of the lasagne and apples in the same way, sprinkling the walnuts in with the other ingredients.

4. Top the final layer of lasagne with the breadcrumbs, and dot with the margarine (if liked add some more cinnamon and a few chopped nuts to the crumbs).

5. Bake at 350°F/180°C (Gas Mark 4) for about 20 minutes, or until cooked and golden. Serve hot.

INDEX